DAILY DEVOTIONAL

CURTIS ESTES, ETHAN FREY,
AND TONY STACY

I AM Daily Devotional
Copyright © 2022 by Curtis R. Estes, Ethan Frey, and Tony Stacy

Published by Bigger Futures Press
An Intellectual Capital Corporation Company

Cover design by Kendra Cagle, 5 Lakes Design

All rights reserved

ISBN: 9798784065636

DEAR READER:

This book is about inviting you into fellowship with us, with your friends, and with God. We are three guys who have texted each other our "I Am" statements every day for six years without fail (nearly). We find a truth from Scripture and commit to embodying this truth for the entire day.

"I Am peace" means that one of us seeks to embody peace; "I Am love" means another seeks to embody love.

We borrowed this idea from the greatest "I Am" statement of all: When Moses asked God who He was, the Lord God responded, *"I AM That I AM"* (Exodus 3:14).

This fellowship has blessed us immeasurably. We now want to share that blessing with you. Each page in this devotional has just one or a few simple "I Am" statements pulled from our text messages to help get you thinking about your own "I Am" statement for the day.

Unlike most books, we encourage you to write in this one. We have provided open space so you can write out your own daily "I Am" statements and join us.

We pray that you ARE and WILL BE all that you focus on from Scripture each day.

All our blessings,
—*Curtis, Ethan, and Tony*

INTRODUCTION
BY CURTIS ESTES

Ethan and Tony had been sharing their favorite Bible verse from their daily morning study for more than a year when I learned of their brotherly collaboration. I was so inspired and hoped that they would allow me to join. Four years later, I'm blown away by the incredible encouragement this practice has been to my life.

I refer to this as a collaboration because together we are better. Every morning I am reminded that I am not running this race alone but have partners who love me, and whom I love, that not only have my back but also want God's very best for me.

The power of declaring "I Am" statements comes straight from the Bible, where we see it over and over. I need this power because we are in a battle for the control of our minds. The "world" wants us to take our identity from material possessions, brand labels, and even advertisements that tell us what is most valuable and what we should aspire to be. These messages are so alluring and seductive, but they draw us away from our true identity: our perfect identity as children of God.

I fall short every day, but with Ethan and Tony's morning inspiration, I am encouraged to get up and reorient myself to God's promises and move forward toward my most amazing future with confidence, peace, and joy, despite the challenges along the way.

My hope is that these daily reminders of God's love and promises will enrich your life with a fresh vision for who you truly ARE as a precious child of our Heavenly Father.

Today, I Am grateful.

I Am grateful that you have this book in your hands. The power of receiving your identity from God leads to blessings beyond imagination. We invite you to join in our collaboration by adding your thoughts to each daily devotion, and perhaps inviting friends who encourage you in this wonderful journey as we all become the best version of ourselves.

INTRODUCTION
BY ETHAN FREY

The significance of using "I Am" statements as part of your journey with the Lord cannot be fully understood without considering both the power of *identity* and the power of *declarative statements.*

Identity

We can see the power of identify by looking at Jesus. In Luke 3, God spoke identity over, and into, Jesus, which was so powerful that the devil immediately wanted to undo it by causing Jesus to doubt his identity.

God rises from the waters of baptism, and He says, *"This is my son. In Him I Am well pleased"* (Luke 3:22).

In the next chapter of Luke, the devil comes to Jesus in the wilderness and attemps to break Jesus's identity down, saying, *"If you are really the son of God, tell this stone to become bread"* (Luke 4:3).

"If you really are the son of God," the devil questions, *"throw yourself down from here"* (Luke 4:9).

One of the devil's primary tactics is to get us to doubt our identity. Nevertheless, Jesus refers to God as "My Father" more than 175 times and refers to Himself as a son 65 times.

Knowing who you are, and WHOSE you are, changes everything.

God has a name for each of us—not the name our parents gave us, but one that is written on our and His hands (Revelations). He knows us better than we know ourselves (Psalms 139). For us to get to know ourselves better, in fact, we need to ask Him who we ARE. When we sit with the Lord each day and contemplate our "I Am" statement, we are asking for His guidance.

Maintaining proper identity is about focus.

In Numbers 13, when God says to go explore the land He is giving His people, ten come back saying how small they are (like grasshoppers) next to the inhabitants of the land. By comparing themselves to others, they were getting their identity from other people, and it made them feel weak and insignificant.

But the two that kept their focus on the land that was promised by God came back saying that the land was awesome.

"Let's go get it!" they said, feeling protected, loved, and worthy.

Point being: We need to get our identity from what God says, not from other people, how we compare to them, or what they say or believe to be true.

We also need to avoid placing our identity in anything else. When Jesus said to the rich young man, "Give away everything you have and follow me" what happened?

"The man went away sad, for he had great wealth" (Matthew 19:12).

His identity was tied to his wealth.

Many people today still mistake their net worth for their self-worth.

Still others get their identities from their sexuality. The Bible instructs us to avoid certain sexual activities because they will distort our identities. If our sexuality, for any reason, occupies too important a place in our identity framework, then it mutes God's ability to speak identity over us.

And there are so many Godly attributes in the Bible—enough for you to see and latch onto something new every day: courage, fearlessness, unshaken-ability, listening, obeying, responding, sensitivity to the Spirit, loved, adored, prized, highly-valued, a son, a daughter, a prince, a friend, blessed, favored, chosen, provided for, in want of nothing, grateful, thankful, richly satisfied, united with, joined together, one.

Like a diamond, there are so many facets to God, and each looks different in different light. You can literally never run out of new things to see. Everyday there are so many ways to let the text wash over and shape you.

Interact with it, respond to it, encounter God in it, and emerge ready to declare the identity He has for you this day!

Sometimes, I will BE the same thing for a week. In fact, this past week, I was patience almost every day. I lately feel as if God is highlighting patience as very important to my sanctification process. The definition of love in 1 Corinthians 13 starts with "Love is patient," and everything that follows patient is impossible. That's why Paul put patience first. It is primary to everything else. The point is, you will go wherever He leads, even in your "I Am" journey.

Lastly, I believe that when we truly know our identity, we become more humble—humble enough to serve. In John 13:3, we see the most towering statement of identity in all the Bible, followed by an incredible act of service:

"Jesus knew that the Father had put all things under his power, and that he had come from God and was returning to God; so he got up from the meal, took off his outer clothing, and wrapped a towel around his waist. After that, he poured water into a basin and began to wash his disciples' feet, drying them with the towel that was wrapped around him."

Declarative Statements

The power of declaring your "I Am" statements is absolutely key because words exist for more than just communicating with others. They are for creation. All of God's creation over the first six days happened by God's spoken word (i.e., "Let there be light, and there was light."). In the Psalms it says that God "spoke the stars into the sky."

And it's not just God who uses the power of declarative statements. Jesus said to a man who had been crippled, "Pick up your mat and get up." Before Jesus declared those words, the man could not have done that. But Jesus' words actually reorganized the world into a new reality, one in which the man could suddenly do what Jesus declared.

Jesus tells us we can do these things and even more. We can tell a mountain to move, and it will.

Now, this book is not to suggest we can all move mountains with our words. But this book is absolutely and unequivocally saying that our words are powerful, and creative, and that they can manifest changes in our worlds.

We need to activate our faith by using declarative statements.

David declared to Goliath, "I am going to cut off your head with your own sword."

Guess what happened.

Even the devil knows the power of declarations. He tempted Jesus to tell the stones to become bread. While Jesus declined, there was nevertheless an acknowledgement that His words had the power to change stones into bread.

So let us do this. Let us have the faith to declare who we are, each day, and then try to live it out.

A few examples from my own experience:

- One day, when I was very troubled about my personal circumstances, I observed that the broader circumstances were also troubling. I had a cold, an issue at work, one of my teenage kids had made a poor choice, and my wife and I were not in agreement on how to handle the child and the consequences of the poor decision.

    That morning, I found in Psalms 29: "The Lord twists the mighty oaks and strips the forest bare, and inside the temple everyone yells glory."

    It hit me instantly. The world around me seemed so twisted. But I Am His. I Am one who goes to the Temple and celebrates with the people of God. In fact, I am His Temple. And I started yelling "Glory" at the top of my lungs.

I then texted Curtis and Tony:

> ETHAN FREY
>
> "I Am yelling glory. That is who I Am. All day. Moment-by-moment."

It propelled me out of despair and into a posture of unshakeable faith.

- Another time, I was discouraged about a problem that kept recurring. I felt like I had been walking and walking, but instead of ascending the mountain of the Lord, I had been circling the base of it, making no progress. Then I read in the Old Testament that again and again, the people of Israel turned away from God and worshipped other gods; and again and again He forgave them.

  It hit me that we have an "again and again" God. He keeps coming. He keeps forgiving. He never stops. My failures cannot outlast His goodness towards me. That morning I wrote:

  > ETHAN FREY
  >
  > "I Am again and again. I do not quit."

  It blessed me so much to be like God in this way, it gave me resolve. If He is willing to be long-suffering with me, then I can be an again-and-again man in this world as well. I declared it as my identity.

INTRODUCTION
BY TONY STACY

For the past six years, I have been tremendously blessed to be a part of an exchange of text messages on a daily basis each work week with two of the greatest human beings I have ever known: Curtis Estes and Ethan Frey.

The daily exchanges aren't just text messages: they are inspiration, they are powerful and authentic declarations of truth, they are uplifting, they are creative and expanding, they are thought provoking, they are healing and blessing, and much more! These text messages contain our daily "I Am" statements that are aligned with Scripture, and they prompt us to remember who we ARE, Whose we ARE, and who we ARE becoming.

As Curtis alluded to in his introduction, the power of declaring "I Am" comes from Scripture. Here are some of my favorites:

Moses said to God, "Behold, when I come to the Israelites and say to them, 'The God of your fathers (ancestors) has sent me to you,' and they say to me, 'What is His name?' What shall I say to them?" (Exodus 3:13-14).

God's response in verse 14 was off the charts awesome! God said to Moses, "I AM WHO I AM."

He said, "You shall say this to the Israelites, 'I AM has sent me to you.'"

This statement of who He IS leaves nothing out, it means all things possible, it tells me that whomever or whatever I may need Him to be, He IS—without limits.

In the book of John, Jesus made some of the most powerful "I AM" statements ever made:

- "*I AM the Resurrection and the Life.*"
- "*I AM the Good Shepherd.*"
- "*I AM the Light of the world.*"

Are words powerful? Indeed they are. A good friend of mine once shared this thought with me: *The words that follow I Am follow you.*

I love being able to declare who I Am, what I Am, Whose I Am, who I Am becoming.

God created the universe with words. Using the word "let," and BOOM, creation began. In Isaiah 55:11, He reminds us of the power in His words: "So will My word be which goes out of My mouth; It will not return to Me void, without accomplishing what I desire, and without succeeding in the matter for which I sent it."

Whoa! This is a power-packed promise of truth, and I love it!

Lastly, we have this same power as He lives and breathes in us. Proverbs 18:21 tells us: "Death and life are in the power of the tongue, and those who love it and indulge it will eat its fruit and bear the consequences of their words."

I thank Curtis and Ethan for allowing me to be a part of their daily "I Am" statements. There have been countless days where they have inspired me, uplifted my spirits, blessed me, healed me, and challenged me.

My hope is that this devotional will uplift, inspire, heal, bless, and challenge you. Join us, we can lift up all of mankind one heartfelt, powerful, declaration of "I Am" at a time.

JANUARY 1

I AM CONSECRATED

CURTIS

I've decided to take the word "consecration" as my word for the year. I want to be wholly consecrated, setting myself apart for use by our Lord. Here's a good reason why ...

"Joshua told the people, 'Consecrate yourselves, for tomorrow the Lord will do amazing things among you'" (Joshua 3:5).

I Am consecrated, all year long!

TONY

Curtis, powerful words to kick off this year. Thank you, brother! You ARE consecrated. Your life is your proof.

ETHAN

Curtis, wonderful stuff! I love consecrated. I see you BEING consecrated every day. You ARE.

HOW ABOUT YOU?

Today, I Am...

JANUARY 2

I AM PEACE

ETHAN

> Mark 4:39 is famous: "When Jesus woke up, he rebuked the wind and said to the waves, 'Silence! Be still!' Suddenly the wind stopped and there was a great calm."
>
> When the inner man is at peace, the outer storms don't matter. We live from the inside out, not the outside in. In fact, we only have authority over the storms we can sleep through!
>
> So today, all day long, I Am peace. And I will live today from that place of peace, regardless of the storms around me. That is who I Am today. Love you guys.

HOW ABOUT YOU?

> Today, I Am...

JANUARY 3

I AM TRUST

TONY

> I have always loved Proverbs 3:5-6, I made TRUST my word of the year!
>
> "Trust in the Lord with all your heart and lean not on your own understanding; in all your ways submit to Him, and He will make your paths straight."
>
> This is very familiar to all, but word-for-word, it is so powerful.
>
> Then I read Psalms 40:4 today: "Blessed is the one who trusts in the Lord."
>
> I see "trust" in both readings. I Am trust today.

ETHAN

> Love it. You ARE trust today. I affirm that. Already prayed for you both today.

CURTIS

> Love you guys.

HOW ABOUT YOU?

> Today, I Am...

JANUARY 4

I AM PATIENT, BRAVE, AND COURAGEOUS

ETHAN

Psalms 27:14

"Wait patiently for the Lord.
Be brave and courageous.
Yes, wait patiently for the Lord."

I Am patient, brave and courageous!

HOW ABOUT YOU?

Today, I Am...

JANUARY 5

I AM LOVE, PEACE, AND TRANSFORMED

ETHAN

Today's I Am statement for me is simple. Jesus says, "This is my command, love each other" (John 15:17).

I'm doing as I'm told today. I Am love. All day long: Love, love, love.

TONY

I love it :) My reading was John 16:33, "I have told you these things, so that in me you may have peace."

I Am peace ... all day long.

CURTIS

My brothers, "Do not conform any longer to the pattern of this world, but be transformed by the renewing of your mind. Then you will be able to test and approve what God's will is—His good, pleasing and perfect will" (Romans 12:2).

I Am transformed, living in His perfect will.

ETHAN

Yeah, Curtis, I love it. That's who you are today! Live it out, Mr. Transformed. The world will be different because of you!

With peace, love and transformed walking together on this planet, the world WILL be better. Imagine what happens when we work together.

HOW ABOUT YOU?

Today, I Am...

JANUARY 6

I AM STILL

ETHAN

"Do not be afraid. Stand firm and you will see the deliverance the Lord will bring you today ... The Lord will fight for you; you need only to be still" (Exodus 14:13-14).

I have relied on this promise many times, so very powerful word-by-word. Take it throughout your day and be blessed.

Today, I Am still.

HOW ABOUT YOU?

Today, I Am...

JANUARY 7

I AM HIS STUDENT

CURTIS

> "I will instruct you and teach you in the way you should go; I will guide you with My eye" (Psalms 32:8).
>
> I Am His student all day long and everyday going forward!

ETHAN

> You ARE His student ... all day long and always. I declare all three of us shall enjoy living out our wonderful identities today.

HOW ABOUT YOU?

Today, I Am...

JANUARY 8

I AM INDESTRUCTIBLE, RIGHTEOUS

ETHAN

Morning, boys. Today I Am indestructible.

"A river brings joy to the city of our God, the sacred home of the most high. God dwells in that city; it cannot be destroyed" (Psalms 46:4-5).

Today, the home of the "most high" is ME. He dwells in me. So I am that city, and I cannot be destroyed. I Am indestructible, all day long.

I have prayed a prayer of blessing over each of you today. God is going to do big things!

TONY

"For the eyes of The Lord are on the righteous and his ears are attentive to their prayer" (1 Peter 3:12).

I Am righteous ... all day long!

Men, have a blessed Monday!

HOW ABOUT YOU?

Today, I Am...

JANUARY 9

I AM GUIDED

CURTIS

"Yet I am always with you; you hold me by my right hand. You guide me with your counsel, and afterward you will take me into glory" (Psalms 73:23-24).

Today, I Am guided all day long. I don't want to do or think anything that hasn't passed through the filter of His leading.

HOW ABOUT YOU?

Today, I Am...

JANUARY 10

I AM A BUILDER OF HUMANS

ETHAN

Paul writes, "We must not just please ourselves. We should help others do what is right and build them up in the Lord" (Romans 15:1-2).

I Am a builder of humans, lifting them higher, helping them, raising their spirits, giving them resources from that which God first gave me, aiding them in casting a higher vision, and elevating their lives. Today, I Am a builder, all day long. That's who I Am.

TONY

You ARE a builder. Love it.

HOW ABOUT YOU?

Today, I Am...

JANUARY 11

I AM STANDING FIRM

TONY

"Thanks be to God! He gives us the victory through our Lord Jesus Christ ... stand firm. Let nothing move you. Always give yourselves fully to the work of the Lord, because you know that your labor in the Lord is not in vain" (1 Corinthians 15:57-58).

Exodus 14:13, "Stand firm and you will see the deliverance the Lord will bring you today."

I Am standing firm today ...

Bless you both today.

CURTIS

Thank you, my brothers! May the Lord bless you and keep you, may the Lord cause His face to shine upon you and give you peace.

HOW ABOUT YOU?

Today, I Am...

JANUARY 12

I AM ENDURANCE

CURTIS

"Therefore we also, since we are surrounded by so great a cloud of witnesses, let us lay aside every weight, and the sin which so easily ensnares us, and let us run with endurance the race that is set before us, looking unto Jesus, the author and finisher of our faith, who for the joy that was set before Him endured the cross, despising the shame, and has sat down at the right hand of the throne of God" (Hebrews 12:1-2).

I Am endurance, running the race God has set before me ... all day long!

HOW ABOUT YOU?

Today, I Am...

JANUARY 13

I AM TRUTH

ETHAN

Today, I bring you a Scripture I have never seen before, one which seems pregnant with meaning (which I will seek to discover more fully this week). It is from the lips of Jesus ...

"He says, 'Every teacher of religious law who becomes a disciple in the Kingdom of Heaven is like a homeowner who brings from his storeroom new gems of truth as well as old.'" (Matthew 13:52).

I love this. It honors religious pursuits but invites people into the new covenant; all can come. It even honors the religious teacher's thinking as old gems of truth. But the new gems of truth come to those in the Kingdom of Heaven. That's me! So I can have the truths of old and the new truths that come from Christ, our human model of the living God.

So I Am truth today. All day long. That's who I Am. And I will bring it to the world today—both old and new—for His glory and the world's good.

Loving you guys. I prayed blessing over both of you today.

HOW ABOUT YOU?

Today, I Am...

JANUARY 14

I AM SERVICE

TONY

Thanks for your prayers, brothers. I declare His favor and grace over you guys.

My reading today: "Each of you should use whatever gift you have received to serve others, as faithful stewards of God's grace" (1 Peter 4:10).

I Am service today, which makes me a faithful steward of God's grace.

ETHAN

You ARE service, Tony, all day long! Thank you for the self-emptying identity statement. The world is better because of you today. And it WILL come back to you!

TONY

Thank you, brother!

HOW ABOUT YOU?

Today, I Am...

JANUARY 15

I AM FILLED, HONOR

CURTIS

"I pray that out of his glorious riches he may strengthen you with power through his Spirit in your inner being, so that Christ may dwell in your hearts through faith. And I pray that you, being rooted and established in love, may have power, together with all the saints, to grasp how wide and long and high and deep is the love of Christ, and to know this love that surpasses knowledge—that you may be filled to the measure of all the fullness of God" (Ephesians 3:16-19).

I Am filled with the love of Christ and the fullness (sufficiency) of God all day long!

ETHAN

Yes you are, Curtis, all day long!

TONY

Great, powerful Scripture. You ARE indeed!

"Do you not know that your bodies are temples of the Holy Spirit, who is in you, whom you have received from God? You are not your own, you were bought at a price. Therefore honor God with your bodies" (1 Corinthians 6:19-20).

I Am honor to Him, all day long.

HOW ABOUT YOU?

Today, I Am...

JANUARY 16

I AM OPEN, COMPASSION, DELIGHTED

ETHAN

Today, I Am open. Just as Jesus opened blind eyes, and the heavens opened above him, and if we ask the doors shall be opened ... I Am open today, and my heart is fully open. It is who I Am and it is all I will do today.

TONY

"Do not let unwholesome talk come out of your mouths, but only what is helpful for building others up according to their needs, that it may benefit those who listen" (Ephesians 4:29).

This means compassion to me. Today, I will follow His word and all day long I Am compassion.

May you have God's favor and grace all day!

CURTIS

"Delight yourself in the Lord and he will give you the desires of your heart" (Psalms 37:4).

Today I Am delighted in God's gracious, abundant love.

HOW ABOUT YOU?

Today, I Am...

JANUARY 17

I AM LISTENING, UNITY

CURTIS

> "When He has brought out all His own, He goes on ahead of them, and His sheep follow Him because they know His voice" (John 10:4).
>
> I Am listening for His voice, all day long!
>
> Praying that we may more and more hear Jesus with absolute clarity and conviction.

TONY

> Amen! Thank you, Curtis.
>
> Psalms 133:1-3 is for us gents: "Behold, how good and pleasant it is when brothers dwell in unity! ... For there the Lord has commanded the blessing."
>
> I Am unity with you, my brothers, all day long

HOW ABOUT YOU?

> Today, I Am...

JANUARY 18

I AM GIVING

ETHAN

> In John 3:16, we hear the famous words: "For God so loved the world that he gave ... "
>
> Later, in that same chapter (John 3:34), John the Baptist says about Jesus, "He speaks God's words, for God gives him the Spirit without limit."
>
> You can see God is a giver. And that is who I Am today. I Am giving ... all day long.
>
> Love you boys. Let me know if there is anything I can give to you.

HOW ABOUT YOU?

> Today, I Am...

JANUARY 19

I AM GRATITUDE, HIS IMPOSSIBLE

TONY

> "For I know the plans I have for you, declares the Lord, plans to prosper you and not to harm you, plans to give you hope and a future" (Jeremiah 29:11).
>
> This is a promise for each of us today. You both will prosper today. It is His plan for you.
>
> I Am gratitude today ... all day long.

CURTIS

> "For nothing is impossible with God" (Luke 1:37).
>
> I Am His impossible all day long.
>
> Let us do the impossible today according to God's power and plan.

HOW ABOUT YOU?

> Today, I Am...

JANUARY 20

I AM LOYAL

CURTIS

"For the eyes of the Lord run to and fro throughout the whole earth, to show Himself strong on behalf of those whose heart is loyal to Him" (2 Chronicles 16:9).

I Am loyal to our Heavenly Father and praise Him for showing Himself strong on my behalf, all day long!

This was too good not to share.

ETHAN

Love the identity statement. Way to go! You ARE loyal, and your loyalty doesn't take a day off! Amen, brother.

TONY

I love that verse! Thanks for sharing. I am joining you; I Am loyal to Him too, all day long.

HOW ABOUT YOU?

Today, I Am...

JANUARY 21

I AM LIFE

ETHAN

One of my favorite verses: "The same Spirit of God who raised Jesus from the dead lives in you!" (Romans 8:13).

So inside of ME, and YOU, is that power to cross over from death to life ... after death has occurred. We have the power to re-write the story, reverse the irreversible.

Today, I Am life. Jesus said, "I AM the way, the truth, and the life" (John 14:6). So this was an identity statement for Jesus as well.

And I believe entailed in this identity statement is the powerful force to break death, despair, depression, doom, fear, failure (etc.), and replace it all with life, abundance, and joy.

So, today, all day long, I Am life.

HOW ABOUT YOU?

Today, I Am...

JANUARY 22

I AM SUREFOOTED

CURTIS

> "Even though the fig trees have no blossoms, and there are no grapes on the vines; even though the olive crop fails, and the fields lie empty and barren; even though the flocks die in the fields, and the cattle barns are empty, yet I will rejoice in the Lord! I will be joyful in the God of my salvation! The Sovereign Lord is my strength! He makes me as surefooted as a deer, able to tread upon the heights" (Habakkuk 3:17-19).
>
> This is a compelling verse in which Habakkuk's feelings were not controlled by the events around him but by faith in God's ability to give him strength. Even in times of starvation and loss, he would still rejoice in the Lord. Nothing made sense and troubles seemed more than he could bear, but he remembered that it was God who gave him strength. Let us take our eyes off our difficulties and look to God.
>
> For this reason, I Am excited to be surefooted, treading upon the heights, all day long!

ETHAN

> That blessed my soul, Curtis. You ARE surefooted! All day long!

HOW ABOUT YOU?

> Today, I Am...

JANUARY 23

I AM FREE, PRAISE

ETHAN

Good morning, mighty men. Today, I have a wonderful identity statement. Not sure if it is the first time I've said this one, but I think so. I Am free.

"Give your burdens to the Lord, and he will take care of you. He will not permit the godly to slip and fall" (Psalms 55:22).

I've given Him my burdens. He has to carry them. And I Am free!

"Cast all your cares on Him because He cares for you" (1 Peter 5:7).

So they are His problems, not mine!

Today, all day long, I Am free ... and light as a feather! His burden is easy. His yoke is light. And whom the Son sets free is free indeed. And that's me!

TONY

Morning brothers! Psalms 56:4 fits beautifully with I Am free!

"In God, whose word I praise,
In God I trust and am not afraid."

I Am praise all day, and because of my trust in Him, I Am not afraid. No fear. I guess that makes me free.

Amen! We are praise, free ... all day long.

HOW ABOUT YOU?

Today, I Am...

JANUARY 24

I AM HIS FAVOR

TONY

"In the time of my favor I heard you, and in the day of salvation I helped you" (2 Corinthians 6:2).

Paul then writes, in the next line, "Now is the time of God's favor ... "

Today, for all three of us, now is the time for His favor.

I Am His favor ... all day long!

You gents have a blessed day. Let me know if I can do anything for either of you.

ETHAN

You ARE His favor today, all day long!

TONY

And so ARE you, Curtis, too.

HOW ABOUT YOU?

Today, I Am...

JANUARY 25

I AM HELD FAST

CURTIS

"Where can I go from your Spirit? Where can I flee from your presence? If I go up to the heavens, you are there; if I make my bed in the depths, you are there. If I rise on the wings of the dawn, if I settle on the far side of the sea, even there your hand will guide me, your right hand will hold me fast" (Psalms 139:7-10).

I Am held fast by the Holy Spirit, all day long.

HOW ABOUT YOU?

Today, I Am...

JANUARY 26

I AM MUSIC

ETHAN

Today, I look to 1 Chronicles 25 for my identity statement. David has selected his army commanders and now, in this chapter, he appoints 288 musicians to "proclaim God's messages ... as they made music at the house of the Lord."

For those people, their role and identity was to make music, playing the Psalms that poured from David's heart.

Today, I Am music. He's put a new song in my mouth, and I will live it out. In fact, I will take all my other identity statements and be toe-tapping to them today ... because today I Am music. All day long.

TONY

> You ARE music all day. Toe tapping all day. :)

HOW ABOUT YOU?

> Today, I Am...

JANUARY 27

I AM WATCHED OVER

CURTIS

"I am with you and will watch over you wherever you go, and I will bring you back to this land. I will not leave you until I have done what I have promised you" (Genesis 28:15).

I Am watched over all day long. And our precious families are watched over, too!

TONY

You ARE indeed watched over, Curtis. That is a fact, my friend!

You are also prayed over!

HOW ABOUT YOU?

Today, I Am...

JANUARY 28

I AM CONTROL, DELIGHTED
ETHAN

> After Cain's gift was rejected by God, he talked to Cain and gave him advice about doing what is right. And, in Genesis 4:7, He says, "Sin is crouching at the door, eager to control you. But you must subdue it and be its master."
>
> So today, I Am control. I understand there is no neutral position: Either you control it, or it controls you. And I Am control. All day long!
>
> Loving you both today and in prayer.

CURTIS

> "Trust in the LORD and do good;
> dwell in the land and enjoy safe pasture.
> Delight yourself in the LORD
> and he will give you the desires of your heart" (Psalms 37:3-4).
>
> I Am delighted today.

HOW ABOUT YOU?

Today, I Am...

JANUARY 29

I AM HOPE, CHRIST-FILLED

TONY

The Scripture is so powerful. A very familiar verse to us all: "But those who hope in the Lord will renew their strength. They will soar on wings like eagles; they will run and not be weary, they will walk and not faint" (Isaiah 40:31).

I Am hope all day ... and I accept His promises from His Word.

May His favor be with you both all day.

ETHAN

Thank you, brother. You ARE hope.

CURTIS

"To them God has chosen to make known among the Gentiles the glorious riches of this mystery, which is Christ in you, the hope of glory" (Colossians 1:27).

I Am Christ-filled all day long.

HOW ABOUT YOU?

Today, I Am...

JANUARY 30

I AM PEACE, COMFORT

CURTIS

"Peace I leave with you; my peace I give you. I do not give to you as the world gives. Do not let your hearts be troubled and do not be afraid" (John 14:27).

I Am peace ... filled up with it and overflowing to those around me.

Receive His peace, my friends!

ETHAN

Yes, you ARE peace. All day long. I receive it. Thanks, buddy.

TONY

"Praise be to the God and Father of our Lord Jesus Christ, the Father of compassion and the God of all comfort, who comforts us in all our troubles, so that we can comfort those in any trouble" (2 Corinthians 1:3-4)

I Am comfort today to any who are in trouble. All day long!

ETHAN

Love it, brother!

HOW ABOUT YOU?

Today, I Am...

JANUARY 31

I AM PRAISE

ETHAN

But when I am afraid, I will put my trust in You. I will praise God for what He has promised" (Psalms 56:3-4).

His promises are bigger than our circumstances! So when we feel afraid, we put our trust in God. And, as David acknowledged, the best way to do that is to praise God. Praise is a mighty weapon. I'm pretty sure it's impossible to have fear while praising God.

And that's what we'll be doing in Heaven for all eternity—wave after wave—so why not bring heaven to earth ("thy kingdom come, on earth as it is in heaven") and praise him now ... all day long?

So I Am praise. That's who I Am. And I will praise the Lord today.

HOW ABOUT YOU?

Today, I Am...

FEBRUARY 1

I AM INSUFFICIENT

CURTIS

Today I rejoice in my insufficiency, knowing that His power is made perfect in weakness.

"Consider it pure joy, my brothers, whenever you face trials of many kinds" (James 1:2).

"And He said to me, 'My grace is sufficient for you, for My strength is made perfect in weakness.' Therefore most gladly I will rather boast in my infirmities, that the power of Christ may rest upon me" (2 Corinthians 12:9).

Today I Am insufficient, but progressing toward His perfection, all day long.

HOW ABOUT YOU?

Today, I Am...

FEBRUARY 2

I AM STEADFAST

ETHAN

> For a very long time, my life verse was Psalms 112:7: "He has no fear of bad news whose heart is steadfast, trusting in the Lord."
>
> So today I return to this Scripture like an old friend and say I Am steadfast. All day long. That's who I Am. And I declare that I will be steadfast in praying for both of you today.

HOW ABOUT YOU?

Today, I Am...

FEBRUARY 3

I AM NEW, PRAYERFUL

TONY

My "I Am" today comes from Isaiah 43:18-19: "Remember not the former things, nor consider the things of old. Behold, I am doing a new thing; now it springs forth."

I Am new, and I will allow Him to spring forth from me today ... all day long!

May you guys have a supernaturally favored day!

ETHAN

I LOVE new. Awesome. And, yes, you ARE new ... all day long.

CURTIS

"Be joyful always; pray continually; give thanks in all circumstances, for this is God's will for you in Christ Jesus" (1 Thessalonians 5:16-18).

I Am prayerful, all day long.

HOW ABOUT YOU?

Today, I Am...

FEBRUARY 4

I AM UNITED WITH CHRIST
CURTIS

"My prayer is not for them alone. I pray also for those who will believe in me through their message, that all of them may be one, Father, just as You are in me and I am in You. May they also be in us so that the world may believe that You have sent me. I have given them the glory that You gave me, that they may be one as we are one: I in them and You in me. May they be brought to complete unity to let the world know that You sent me and have loved them even as You have loved me" (John 17:20-23).

I Am united with Christ, and Ethan and Tony, all day long!

HOW ABOUT YOU?

Today, I Am...

FEBRUARY 5

I AM LETTING GO

ETHAN

> "We know what real love is because Jesus gave up his life for us. So we also ought to give up our lives for our brothers and sisters" (1 John 3:16).
>
> I Am letting go and experiencing the joy and freedom of the life surrendered! Hallelujah!

HOW ABOUT YOU?

Today, I Am…

FEBRUARY 6

I AM BLESSING

TONY

> This morning, the blessing spoken by Aaron in Numbers 6:24-26, I claim for the three of us today and everybody we come in contact with: "The Lord bless you and keep you; the Lord make his face to shine upon you and be gracious to you; the Lord lift up his face upon you and give you peace."
>
> I Am this blessing all day long! And so are both of you.

HOW ABOUT YOU?

> Today, I Am...

FEBRUARY 7

I AM CONSUMED

CURTIS

"Therefore, since we are receiving a kingdom that cannot be shaken, let us be thankful, and so worship God acceptably with reverence and awe, for our God is a consuming fire" (Hebrews 12:28-29).

I want to go deeper with Jesus. Today I Am consumed by the fire of God's desire for me to know Jesus, all day long!

HOW ABOUT YOU?

Today, I Am...

FEBRUARY 8

I AM BOLD LOVE

ETHAN

In Mark 3, the Pharisees planned on accusing Jesus of working on the Sabbath if he healed someone. So Jesus brought a man with a deformed hand up to the front of the synagogue and turned to His critics and said: "Does the law permit good deeds on the Sabbath, or is it a day for doing evil? Is this a day to save life or to destroy it?"

Jesus knew His Father's nature is love and life, and His nature doesn't take a day off. In fact, Jesus would stand up in a room full of critics to love me! His intentions for me are always loving and good. I literally can't escape it.

Today, I Am bold love.

HOW ABOUT YOU?

Today, I Am...

FEBRUARY 9

I AM FAITH

TONY

"For He has said, 'I will never leave you nor forsake you,' so we can confidently say, 'The Lord is my helper; I will not fear'" (Hebrews 13:6).

This is a week of faith. I choose faith over fear. I Am faith today. All day long.

ETHAN

Thank you, Tony! You ARE faith and it conquers all fear.

HOW ABOUT YOU?

Today, I Am...

FEBRUARY 10

I AM HUMBLY PATIENT

CURTIS

"Humble yourselves, therefore, under God's mighty hand, that he may lift you up in due time. Cast all your anxiety on him because he cares for you" (1 Peter 5:6-7).

I Am humbly patient, all day long, waiting for God to lift me up in His perfect timing.

HOW ABOUT YOU?

Today, I Am...

FEBRUARY 11

I AM CONFIDENCE, FAITHFULLY OBEDIENT, TRUSTING

ETHAN

Today, my identity statement is a spin-off of faith: "Faith is the confidence that what we hope for will actually happen" (Hebrews 11:1). So today I Am confidence. And I will be confident in the unseen things all day long!

TONY

Morning, gents! Thank you for the promise of Hebrews 11:1. I needed that. I love it, and you ARE confidence today, all day, brother.

Deuteronomy 28:1-2 says, "And if you faithfully [there is that word again] obey the voice of the Lord your God ... all these blessings shall come upon you and overtake you."

I Am faithfully obedient today. His blessings and favor will chase me down and overtake me. Awesome.

CURTIS

Here's to being chased down by blessings and favor!

"O Lord Almighty, blessed is the man who trusts in you" (Psalms 84:12). I Am trusting our Almighty Lord, all day long.

HOW ABOUT YOU?

Today, I Am...

FEBRUARY 12

I AM PURIFIED

CURTIS

> "But if we walk in the light, as He is in the light, we have fellowship with one another, and the blood of Jesus, his Son, purifies us from all sin" (1 John 1:7).
>
> I Am purified, walking in the light of Jesus, all day long.
>
> I've prayed for you both this morning. Can't wait to see how God will act in our lives today.

ETHAN

> Morning, men. Thank you, Curtis! Purified is awesome. I've prayed for you both, all your affairs, and may He abundantly breathe His Favor into your lives today.

HOW ABOUT YOU?

Today, I Am...

FEBRUARY 13

I AM DESPERATE (FOR HIM)
ETHAN

As believers, we can feel safe in the shelter of His wings. And that's true. But I think God loves when we come to Him in anguish as well.

Psalms 77:2-3 says: "When I was in deep trouble, I searched for the Lord. All night long I lifted my hands toward heaven, but my soul was not comforted. I think of God, and I moan, overwhelmed with longing for His help."

Obviously, this is not the warm fuzzy stuff. This is the stuff of contending, and it honors God. These are the words of those who are in impossible situations and need the God of the impossible to help. Nothing brings the believer out of us like desperate circumstances.

So today I Am desperate (for Him). I need Him to show up and do what only He can.

TONY

> Ethan, with God, all things are possible, which leaves nothing out, and that is a promise straight from the lips of Jesus Christ Himself. :)

HOW ABOUT YOU?

> Today, I Am...

FEBRUARY 14

I AM STRENGTH, UPHELD

TONY

In 2 Tim 4:17, Paul wrote, "The Lord stood by me and strengthened me."

Today, I Am strength, all day long brothers.

CURTIS

"If the Lord delights in a man's way,
he makes his steps firm;
though he stumble, he will not fall,
for the Lord upholds him with his hand" (Psalms 37:23-24).

I Am upheld, all day long! Let's live in God's delight my brothers.

ETHAN

Awesome, Curtis.

You ARE upheld, all day long. And that's a great identity you've chosen for today.

HOW ABOUT YOU?

Today, I Am...

FEBRUARY 15

I AM CHOSEN

ETHAN

> "Just as He chose us in Him before the foundation of the world, that we should be holy and without blame before Him in love" (Ephesians 1:4).
>
> Today I Am chosen all day long, living a holy life with the power of the Holy Spirit and blameless in God's eyes through my redemption in Christ.

HOW ABOUT YOU?

> Today, I Am...

FEBRUARY 16

I AM GLAD

ETHAN

> Good morning, boys. God told me this is going to be a very good week for all of us. So gear up. I'm praying for you both.
>
> 1 Peter 1:6 says, "So be truly glad. There is wonderful joy ahead."
>
> Today, I'm taking Peter's advice: I Am truly glad. Most of the circumstances in my life are temporary, but not God's presence. His love is mine forever. His promises are mine forever. His great goodness is mine forever.
>
> Today, my identity acknowledges these eternal truths and proclaims, "I Am truly glad." All day long!

TONY

> Morning, gentlemen. Thank you, Ethan, for your prayers. I am praying for you gents as well and I accept Ethan's declaration about our week! Supernatural favor!
>
> You ARE glad! Love it! God wants us to be happy. It is His will. We are to bring happiness to all who look upon us.

HOW ABOUT YOU?

> Today, I Am...

FEBRUARY 17

I AM HIS UNFAILING LOVE
CURTIS

"'Though the mountains be shaken and the hills be removed, yet my unfailing love for you will not be shaken nor my covenant of peace be removed,' says the Lord, who has compassion on you" (Isaiah 54:10).

Today I Am His unfailing love, all day long!

HOW ABOUT YOU?

Today, I Am...

FEBRUARY 18

I AM A GUARDIAN

ETHAN

> The Bible warns us in Proverbs to guard our hearts: "Above all else, guard your heart, for everything you do flows from it."
>
> Today, I Am a guardian. Let no unrighteous thing penetrate my heart, my mind, the boundaries of my property, or my conversations. I will stand on the watchtower for my family, my friends, as well as myself. For I Am a GUARDIAN!

TONY

> This is awesome! I love that Scripture in Proverbs.

HOW ABOUT YOU?

> Today, I Am...

FEBRUARY 19

I AM LIGHT

TONY

I very much look forward to God's word every morning, His guidance for my day, and I am also thankful I have you boys sharing your ministry with me daily—a true blessing to me.

John 8:12 provides my "I am" statement today. Jesus spoke, "I am the light of the world. Whoever follows me will not walk in darkness, but will have the light of life."

I Am light ... for others to see, all day long!

ETHAN

You ARE light, Tony! That has been part of your identity from the time you were born up to this very day! Thank you for the light of your prayer and wisdom on my life. It is a blessing to me.

TONY

Thank you, my friend!

HOW ABOUT YOU?

Today, I Am...

FEBRUARY 20

I AM HELD BY MY HEAVENLY FATHER

CURTIS

"For I AM the Lord, your God, who takes hold of your right hand and says to you, 'Do not fear; I will help you'" (Isaiah 41:13).

Today I Am held by my heavenly Father, and so are you!

ETHAN

You are heavenly held today, Curtis.

HOW ABOUT YOU?

Today, I Am...

FEBRUARY 21

I AM DOING HIS WORK

ETHAN

Reading 2 Samuel 7 today. The entire chapter is awesome as it contains the Lord's Covenant with David and David's prayer of gratitude in return. I am taking one verse today, verse 3, and claiming it as my own.

"Go, do all that is in your heart, for the Lord is with you" (2 Samuel 7:3).

I believe the desires of my heart were placed there by God and I am pursuing them. Today I Am doing His work all day.

HOW ABOUT YOU?

Today, I Am...

FEBRUARY 22

I AM ROOTED AND BUILT UP

CURTIS

> "So then, just as you received Christ Jesus as Lord, continue to live in Him, rooted and built up in Him, strengthened in the faith as you were taught, and overflowing with thankfulness" (Colossians 2:6-7).
>
> I love the idea of our roots going deep into the ground for stability and being built up in strength so that we can be used by God for His glorious purpose in this world.
>
> Today I Am rooted and built up in Christ Jesus all day long.

TONY

> I love it. The taller the building, the deeper the foundation. The taller we stand, the deeper our roots need to be. You ARE rooted and built up all day, Curtis!

HOW ABOUT YOU?

Today, I Am...

FEBRUARY 23

I AM GRACIOUS, PERFECT PEACE

ETHAN

Today, I move one more step down the definition of love in 1 Corinthians 13. "Love is not rude" (NLT) or "unmannerly" (Amp). The opposite of rude is "polite, courteous, gracious."

So I Am gracious. I will live in the moment and be polite and nice to everyone with whom I come into contact today. All day long.

CURTIS

"You will keep him in perfect peace,
Whose mind is stayed on You,
Because he trusts in You" (Isaiah 26:3).

I Am His perfect peace all day long.

HOW ABOUT YOU?

Today, I Am...

FEBRUARY 24

I AM BLESSED

TONY

> My reading was in John 20, and my identity comes from verse 29 when Jesus spoke, "Blessed are those who have not seen and yet have believed."
>
> Today, I Am blessed all day long. And if I Am blessed, so are both of you.

ETHAN

> Thank you, brother Tony. You ARE blessed. All day long.

CURTIS

> "Taste and see that the LORD is good;
> blessed is the man who takes refuge in him" (Psalms 34:8).
>
> I Am blessed too, taking refuge in Him, all day long.

HOW ABOUT YOU?

> Today, I Am...

FEBRUARY 25

I AM THE LORD'S SONG

CURTIS

"Surely God is my salvation; I will trust and not be afraid. The Lord, the Lord, is my strength and my song; he has become my salvation" (Isaiah 12:2).

Today, I Am the Lord's song. He fills my heart with music, and I live in this world, but not of this world, as He shows me the glory of His almighty plan.

ETHAN

Amen and amen, my good brother. Enjoy the music of His song—which is you!—today.

HOW ABOUT YOU?

Today, I Am...

FEBRUARY 26

I AM FAITH, KNOWN

ETHAN

This simple Scripture hit me today: "Leave your native country, your relatives, and your father's family, and go to the land that I will show you" (Genesis 12:1).

Did you catch that?

"... that I WILL show you."

No wonder Abraham is considered the father of faith. He left everything familiar to him without even knowing where he was going. Today, I Am faith.

CURTIS

You are faith and overflowing encouragement to all of us around you. Thanks brother!

"O Lord, you have searched me and you know me. You know when I sit and when I rise; you perceive my thoughts from afar. You discern my going out and my lying down; you are familiar with all my ways. Before a word is on my tongue You know it completely, O Lord" (Psalms 139:1-4).

I aAm known, with nothing to hide, all day long.

ETHAN

Dude, I love that identity statement. Yes, you ARE known. That is who you are. All day long.

HOW ABOUT YOU?

Today, I Am...

FEBRUARY 27

I AM DOING GOOD WORKS
CURTIS

> "For we are God's workmanship, created in Christ Jesus to do good works, which God prepared in advance for us to do" (Ephesians 2:10).
>
> Today I Am doing good works which God prepared just for me to do.

HOW ABOUT YOU?

Today, I Am...

FEBRUARY 28

I AM STRONG

ETHAN

Good morning, mighty men. Today, I am continuing my reading of Psalms 89 (it's a long one), and I came upon verse 17, talking about the believer:

"It pleases you to make us strong."

It doesn't matter how we're made or how we feel, all throughout the Bible, God uses ordinary men to do amazing things. We just have to trust God and go after His plans for us. God is pleased to make us strong.

And today I receive that, and today I say, I Am strong. (He is my glorious strength!) And even my identity statement today is pleasing to Him. Yay God!

TONY

Yay God, indeed! You are strong and infinitely pleasing to Him.

HOW ABOUT YOU?

Today, I Am...

FEBRUARY 29

I AM UPHELD, PRAYING IN THE HOLY SPIRIT

ETHAN

Good morning. I have circled you again this morning in prayer for key progress. God knows where we need it (better than we do) and he will give us the key progress we need. This morning I paused on this verse about how God is forever changeless... "You, Master, started it all, laid earth's foundations, then crafted the stars in the sky. Earth and sky will wear out, but not you ... you'll stay the same, year after year; you'll never fade, you'll never wear out" (Hebrews 1:10-12).

It reminds me of the powerful hymn; "On Christ the solid rock I stand, all other ground is sinking sand." I Am upheld by his unchanging, unending love.

TONY

Love who you are! Every day, upheld by His unchanging, unending love is pure truth. You guys are circled, His special blessing given to people of Israel chasing you down today in all of your affairs. This I know. This is so beautiful: "But you, beloved, build yourselves up on [the foundation of] your most holy faith [continually progress, rise like an edifice higher and higher], pray in the Holy Spirit, and keep yourselves in the love of God, waiting anxiously and looking forward to the mercy of our Lord Jesus Christ [which will bring you] to eternal life" (Jude 20-21)

I Am praying in the Holy Spirit for us, all day long.

HOW ABOUT YOU?

Today, I Am...

MARCH 1

I AM VICTORY

TONY

> Morning, mighty men! After seeing your text messages this morning, which are uplifting to me, I was reminded of an under-the-radar Scripture I read recently. I thought this was powerful and applicable for all of us: "Not one word of all the good promises that the Lord had made to the house of Israel had failed; all came to pass" (Joshua 21:45).
>
> That is our Father; He keeps ALL promises and doesn't fail. So today, in light of God's invincible faithfulness, I Am victory!

ETHAN

> Tony, I loved your below-the-radar Scripture. It's especially awesome that all His promises come to pass when you think about how there are over 6,000 promises of God in the Bible! We have it made, boys! You are victory, Tony! In work, in marriage, in temptation, in everything! Your life is marked by prosperity, abundance, and victory!
>
> I am praying for you.
>
> Victory for all, now and forever!

HOW ABOUT YOU?

> Today, I Am...

MARCH 2

I AM WANTING GOD'S WILL
TONY

"Going a little ahead, he fell on his face, praying, 'My Father, if there is any way, get me out of this. But please, not what I want. You, what do you want?'" (Matthew 26:39).

Today I Am wanting God's will and deep, satisfied contentment with how He unfolds it before me.

HOW ABOUT YOU?

Today, I Am...

MARCH 3

I AM ONE WITH GOD

ETHAN

> Jesus said to his disciples, "I am the vine; you are the branches. Those who remain in me, and I in them, will produce much fruit" (John 15:5). Then, in verse 7, He says, "If you remain in me and my words remain in you, ask for anything you want and it will be granted!"
>
> Our highest purpose is relationship with God. "For a branch cannot produce fruit if it is severed from the vine" (John 15:4). He created you and me from nothing because He wanted to be in relationship with us, not for what we can do. (He has angels to do that work!) I love that God wants a relationship with me so much that He created me, exactly as I am, so He could enjoy me. That's so good. So, today, I Am one with God. All day long!

HOW ABOUT YOU?

> Today, I Am...

MARCH 4

I AM WEAK

CURTIS

"But he said to me, 'My grace is sufficient for you, for my power is made perfect in weakness.' Therefore I will boast all the more gladly about my weaknesses, so that Christ's power may rest on me" (2 Corinthians 12:9).

I Am weak so that Christ's power can be made perfect in me, trusting these promises all day long.

ETHAN

That's so good, Curtis. Christ's power will rest on you today, all day long!

HOW ABOUT YOU?

Today, I Am...

MARCH 5

I AM HUMBLE

ETHAN

> James 4:6 says that God "opposes the proud but gives grace to the humble." Humility is the magnet that attracts God's favor. God wants to give us more of His favor, but it can only come to a heart of humility. Today, I Am humble; I yield fully to the Potter, knowing that humility is the key to unlock the door of His favor.

HOW ABOUT YOU?

> Today, I Am...

MARCH 6

I AM PURPOSE

TONY

Morning gents, keep me in your prayers.

"Great are your purposes and mighty are your deeds. Your eyes are open to the ways of all mankind; you reward each person according to their conduct and as their deeds deserve" (Jeremiah 32:19). Today, I Am purpose. His purpose. All day long. May your day be filled with favor and mercy.

ETHAN

Morning, Tony. I'm praying for you. Lifting you up high in prayer today in every area of your life. And you are purpose today. That is a great word for you. And being purpose will give you and others many blessings today. Love you, brother.

TONY

Thank you, brother. This is a day of miracles for all of us!!

HOW ABOUT YOU?

Today, I Am...

MARCH 7

I AM GRASPING THE LOVE OF CHRIST

CURTIS

"I pray that out of his glorious riches He may strengthen you with power through His Spirit in your inner being, so that Christ may dwell in your hearts through faith. And I pray that you, being rooted and established in love, may have power, together with all the saints, to grasp how wide and long and high and deep is the love of Christ, and to know this love that surpasses knowledge—that you may be filled to the measure of all the fullness of God" (Ephesians 3:16-19).

Today I Am grasping how wide and long and high and deep is the love of Christ and knowing this love that surpasses understanding!

HOW ABOUT YOU?

Today, I Am...

MARCH 8

I AM STRENGTHENED

ETHAN

> Love these verses from Daniel during a conversation with Gabriel ...
>
> "Then he said, 'Don't be afraid, Daniel. Since the first day you began to pray for understanding and to humble yourself before your God, your request has been heard in heaven. I have come in answer to your prayer.'
>
> "'Don't be afraid,' he said, 'for you are very precious to God. Peace! Be encouraged! Be strong!' As he spoke these words to me, I suddenly felt stronger and said to him, 'Please speak to me, my lord, for you have strengthened me'" (Daniel 10:12-18).
>
> I hear God's promises and I Am strengthened all day long!

HOW ABOUT YOU?

> Today, I Am...

MARCH 9

I AM YOKED

CURTIS

> "Come to me, all you who are weary and burdened, and I will give you rest. Take my yoke upon you and learn from me, for I am gentle and humble in heart, and you will find rest for your souls. For my yoke is easy and my burden is light" (Matthew 11:28-30).
>
> Today I Am yoked with Jesus Christ. He lightens my burdens and keeps me on His perfect path all day long.

TONY

> Awesome, Curtis. You are yoked. And, therefore, you have eyes to see and ears to hear. Enjoy every victory today.

HOW ABOUT YOU?

> Today, I Am...

MARCH 10

I AM SECURE

CURTIS

Good morning. Today I share with you Psalms 94:18: "I cried out 'I am slipping!' but your unfailing love, O Lord, supported me."

We may feel like we're falling down, but His love takes hold of our hand and holds us up. Though we be falling, God's love of us—and all His promises for us—stand upright for all time.

So today I Am secure—as sure-footed as a deer.

HOW ABOUT YOU?

Today, I Am...

MARCH 11

I AM OBEDIENCE, WORKING FOR THE LORD

TONY

> The first fourteen verses of Deuteronomy 28 speak of blessings for obedience—obedience to the voice of God. Numerous promises are made, and I declare those promises for us today.
>
> I Am obedience to His voice all day long.
>
> And I love verse 2: "And all these blessings shall come upon you and overtake you if you obey the voice of the Lord your God."
>
> Chase us down today. Thanks, guys, for your prayers.

CURTIS

> I'm geared up for our week!
>
> "Whatever you do, work at it with all your heart, as working for the Lord, not for men" (Colossians 3:23).
>
> I Am working for the Lord, with all my heart, all day long!

HOW ABOUT YOU?

> Today, I Am...

MARCH 12

I AM CLOTHED IN JESUS CHRIST
CURTIS

> "Rather, clothe yourselves with the Lord Jesus Christ, and do not think about how to gratify the desires of the sinful nature" (Romans 13:14).
>
> "Therefore, as God's chosen people, holy and dearly loved, clothe yourselves with compassion, kindness, humility, gentleness and patience" (Colossians 3:12).
>
> Today, I Am clothed in Jesus Christ, sharing compassion, kindness, humility, gentleness and patience with all those I'm around, all day long.

HOW ABOUT YOU?

Today, I Am...

MARCH 13

I AM A FATHER

ETHAN

> Good morning, amigos. Some of my identity statements seem like things I want to be more than things I currently am. That's fine—nothing wrong with aspirational identity statements.
>
> But today I provide an identity statement that truly is a deep part of who I am.
>
> I Am a father. According to Genesis 17:4, God said Abraham would be "the father of many nations," and said much about Abraham's descendants (from generation to generation). There is a heritage and a timelessness tied up in this. It's inspiring to think that as a father and son relationship unfolds, it is creating a powerful line of descendants with strong identity.
>
> I Am a father today.

HOW ABOUT YOU?

> Today, I Am...

MARCH 14

I AM TRUST IN HIM

TONY

> Bless you both. And today I hold onto His promise in Psalms 65:11: "You crown the year with your goodness, and your paths drip with abundance."
>
> I Am trust in Him today. He makes straight our paths and they drip with abundance. Blessings and peace in abundance.
>
> Bless you both!

HOW ABOUT YOU?

Today, I Am...

MARCH 15

I AM A GOD'S COMPLETE LOVE

CURTIS

> "No one has ever seen God; but if we love one another, God lives in us and His love is made complete in us" (1 John 4:12).
>
> Today I Am God's complete love, and I share it with everyone around me!

TONY

> Curtis, that is a towering statement of you. I love it! And you are God's complete love, always.

HOW ABOUT YOU?

Today, I Am...

MARCH 16

I AM YIELDED

ETHAN

Only as I yield to the Lord in my inner life will my outer life change. God knows I have needs, desires, and ambitions, but He refuses to give them to me if doing so will leave me inwardly the same. He calls me into deeper relationship and uses my desires in the outer world to bring my inner world closer to Him.

"Seek first His kingdom and His righteousness, and all these things will be given to you as well" (Matthew 6:33).

Today, I Am yielded.

HOW ABOUT YOU?

Today, I Am...

MARCH 17

I AM STRONG AND COURAGEOUS
TONY

Moses tells Joshua, "Be strong and courageous, do not fear ... It is The Lord who goes before you; He will be with you; He will not leave you or forsake you" (Deuteronomy 31:6-8).

Three commands, four promises, all rolled into one!

I Am strong and courageous all day! Look out, world.

HOW ABOUT YOU?

Today, I Am...

MARCH 18

I AM ETERNALLY BLESSED

CURTIS

"Surely you have granted him eternal blessings and made him glad with the joy of your presence" (Psalms 21:6).

Today I Am eternally blessed all day and all life long!

TONY

Amen to another day! You are eternally blessed, Curtis. I love that, and I too am blessed, no doubts about that.

HOW ABOUT YOU?

Today, I Am...

MARCH 19

I AM THE SUDDENLY

ETHAN

We all have our own thoughts. And we listen to them, consider them, ponder them, and continue with them until—suddenly—a thought comes from a totally separate place. It wasn't ours. It had nothing to do with our line of thinking. It was the still small voice of God.

"Suddenly the Lord spoke to Moses" (Numbers 12:4).

"Suddenly a sound like the blowing of a violent wind" (Acts 2:2).

"Suddenly a light from heaven flashed around him" (Acts 9:3).

His thoughts are not our thoughts, and they seem to come out of nowhere. Today, I Am the suddenly, and I will hear from God all day long at the precise moment I need to. God is my guide, and He will be with me in the suddenly.

HOW ABOUT YOU?

Today, I Am…

MARCH 20

I AM LOVE

TONY

Gents, hope your day is going well. You have been prayed for and may your day be filled abundantly with miracles.

1 Corinthians 13:2, my word of the week, says, "If I have all faith, so as to remove mountains, but have not love, I am nothing."

But today, I Am love and that, along with my faith, is powerful! Thanks to Him.

ETHAN

You are a powerful example of faith and love, Tony. It's who you ARE. Thanks for the consistency of your uplifting words.

HOW ABOUT YOU?

Today, I Am...

MARCH 21

I AM EXPECTATION

CURTIS

"In the morning, O Lord, you hear my voice; in the morning I lay my requests before you and wait in expectation" (Psalms 5:3).

Today, I Am expectation, knowing that the good Lord is going before us with perfect plans, established before the creation of the earth.

HOW ABOUT YOU?

Today, I Am...

MARCH 22

I AM UNLIMITED

ETHAN

Good morning, my faithful brothers. Here is a verse for us that is fun to ponder: "Even perfection has its limits, but your commands have no limits" (Psalms 119:96).

How could they? He created it all! So today I return to the familiar identity statement: I Am unlimited. And, like His commands, I too cannot be contained. Not even by death.

HOW ABOUT YOU?

Today, I Am...

MARCH 23

I AM THANKSGIVING

TONY

> Here's my reading from Psalms 50:23: "The one who offers thanksgiving as his sacrifice glorifies me."
>
> Today, I Am thanksgiving and I will offer thanks to Him all day long. I'm praying for both of you and all your affairs, and I know He will answer. And I conclude with the words of Jesus: "Father, I thank you that you have heard me" (John 11:41).
>
> Amen!

HOW ABOUT YOU?

> Today, I Am...

MARCH 24

I AM STILL

CURTIS

"Be still and know that I am God; I will be exalted among the nations, I will be exalted in the earth!" (Psalms 46:10).

Today I Am still; I have ceased striving and am wholly abiding in our Father's plan and provision, all day long.

Brothers, praying for you with the peace that surpasses understanding!

HOW ABOUT YOU?

Today, I Am...

MARCH 25

I AM FASCINATED BY MY SAVIOR
ETHAN

> Today I am struck by the simple, final verse of John: "Jesus did many other things. If they were all written down, I suppose the whole world could not contain the books that would be written" (John 21:25).
>
> Think about it; the world is not big enough for all the books! Jesus is flat-out that amazing. I bet some of His best teachings, or greatest miracles, escaped being written down! There is so much more to Jesus than we know.
>
> So today I Am fascinated by my savior—the one who is simultaneously "the source of David and the heir to his throne" (Revelation 22:16).
>
> Who I am is enjoying who HE IS!

HOW ABOUT YOU?

> Today, I Am...

MARCH 26

I AM COURAGEOUS

CURTIS

When the disciples were in the boat amid the storm, Jesus was there. He's always there for all His children, never more so than when they (we) are afraid.

"But Jesus spoke to them at once. 'Don't be afraid,' he said. 'Take courage. I am here!'" (Matthew 14:27).

Today, I Am courageous, not only for myself but also for all those around me who are experiencing difficult times and fear.

HOW ABOUT YOU?

Today, I Am...

MARCH 27

I AM GRATEFUL

ETHAN

> Today the Lord brought me back to one of my favorite verses in all His good word: "How great is the goodness you have stored up for those who fear you" (Psalms 31:19).
>
> Men, when we fear, revere, and worship the Lord, He piles up high goodness and blessings and benefits for us. This is a good word. I claim it for each of us today, and I receive it. Today, I Am grateful for every goodness and blessing He has stacked up high for me.

HOW ABOUT YOU?

> Today, I Am...

MARCH 28

I AM OPEN

CURTIS

> Morning, men. Today my mind is opening up to this well-known Scripture: "I stand at the door and knock; anyone who hears my voice will open the door and I will come in to him and dine with him" (Revelation 3:20).
>
> God wants to have greater relationship with us, but we need to be open. Today, I Am open. He can come in and have full reign of my heart. It's His today.

HOW ABOUT YOU?

Today, I Am...

MARCH 29

I AM FOREVER GUIDED

CURTIS

"For this God is our God for ever and ever; he will be our guide even to the end" (Psalms 48:14).

Today, I Am forever guided, trusting in our Savior's sovereign plan.

TONY

You ARE forever guided all day. And I throw in Isaiah 55:9 today: "For as the heavens are higher than the earth, so are my ways higher than your ways and my thoughts higher than your thoughts."

I'm joining Curtis and I Am guided by Him all day.

HOW ABOUT YOU?

Today, I Am…

MARCH 30

I AM UNDERSTANDING

ETHAN

> This verse is mine for today: "I will pursue your commands, for you expand my understanding" (Psalms 119:32).
>
> Today, I Am understanding; and I will love the world and everyone I come into contact with from a place of deep understanding today—because it's who I Am.

HOW ABOUT YOU?

> Today, I Am...

MARCH 31

I AM REJOICED OVER

CURTIS

> "The Lord your God is with you, He is mighty to save. He will take great delight in you, He will quiet you with His love, He will rejoice over you with singing" (Zephaniah 3:17).
>
> Today I Am rejoiced over by our Heavenly Father, who loves us and wants to encourage us more than we can ever hope for or imagine. I receive His rejoicing today!

TONY

> Love it, Curtis. You ARE rejoiced over all day, and prayed over.

CURTIS

> I'm praying for you both, too. Blessings and favor to you!

HOW ABOUT YOU?

> Today, I Am...

APRIL 1

I AM LOVING SUNLIGHT

ETHAN

I love Matthew 5:43-45: "But I say love your enemies! Pray for those who persecute you! In that way, you will be acting as true children of your Father in heaven. For He gives sunlight to both the evil and the good."

Today, I Am loving sunlight, and I will love enemies and pray for those seeking to hurt me, because they need sunlight all the more. As a bonus, I get to show God that I Am His true child.

CURTIS

Thank you for being loving sunlight in our lives!

HOW ABOUT YOU?

Today, I Am...

APRIL 2

I AM FREE, AN OVERCOMER

TONY

Today I Am free.

"Then you will know the truth, and the truth will set you free" (John 8:32).

So today I Am free: Free to love, serve, encourage, speak truth, succeed, prosper, forgive, and more.

CURTIS

"I have told you these things, so that in me you may have peace. In this world you will have trouble. But take heart! I have overcome the world" (John 16:33).

I Am an overcomer through Christ, all day long. I see challenges as opportunities to depend on God's strength and grow closer to Him.

HOW ABOUT YOU?

Today, I Am...

APRIL 3

I AM CHEERFUL

CURTIS

Good morning, brothers! I hope this note brings a smile to your faces: "A cheerful heart is good medicine, but a crushed spirit dries up the bones" (Proverbs 17:22).

Today I Am cheerful all day long! Know that when we trust God's plan, we can take this life a whole lot less seriously. Take up His light burden and easy yoke and set down the weight of the world.

HOW ABOUT YOU?

Today, I Am...

APRIL 4

I AM PURE SERVICE

TONY

Good morning, men. Pray I serve others well today, loving and helping and giving away prosperity and blessings.

Today I return to a favorite verse: "Christ did not come to be served, but to serve" (Mark 20:28). I Am pure service today. I need nothing back. I just want others to be blessed.

HOW ABOUT YOU?

Today, I Am...

APRIL 5

I AM LED

CURTIS

"O Lord, you have searched me and you know me. You know when I sit and when I rise; you perceive my thoughts from afar. You discern my going out and my lying down; you are familiar with all my ways. Before a word is on my tongue you know it completely, O Lord... Search me, O God, and know my heart; test me and know my anxious thoughts. See if there is any offensive way in me and lead me in the way everlasting" (Psalms 139:1-24).

Today I Am led in the way everlasting, all day long!

HOW ABOUT YOU?

Today, I Am...

APRIL 6

I AM BRINGING FORTH LIFE

ETHAN

> The power of the Holy Spirit is more than just a counselor: "The Spirit alone gives eternal life" (John 6:63).
>
> The power of the Holy Spirit raised Jesus from the dead. It brings forth life. And, today, I Am bringing forth life! I have the Holy Spirit inside of me, and its power will be active today in bringing forth love, life, prosperity, and grace to all I encounter.

TONY

> Ethan, you are bringing forth life, and love, to all you come into contact with today, brother, all day long!

HOW ABOUT YOU?

> Today, I Am...

APRIL 7

I AM INTEGRITY

TONY

Today a verse grabbed a hold of me: "I will lead a life of integrity in my own home" (Psalms 101:2).

I believe this comes down to choices. It's staying committed to a wise lifestyle. It's not just a front you put on in public, but it's who you are at home as well. It's your identity. And it drives who your children become because you model it when no one else is looking.

Integrity: this is my identity today. I Am integrity. It inspires me, and God deserves nothing less. So, too, my wife deserves nothing less. My kids, my friends, my parents, my colleagues—even me: We all deserve nothing less.

HOW ABOUT YOU?

Today, I Am...

APRIL 8

I AM OBEDIENT

CURTIS

"...and teaching them to obey everything I have commanded you. And surely I am with you always, to the very end of the age" (Matthew 28:20).

Today I Am obedient all day long. I just want to stay right in step with the Holy Spirit's leading, moment by moment.

HOW ABOUT YOU?

Today, I Am...

APRIL 9

I AM RELIANT ON HIM

ETHAN

> My reading today was 2 Chronicles 16:9; it is a wonderful promise. A seer tells Asa, "Because you relied on the Lord, he gave them into your hand. For the eyes of the Lord run to and fro throughout the whole earth, to give strong support to those whose heart is blameless toward Him."
>
> I Am reliant on Him, all day, in all ways.

HOW ABOUT YOU?

> Today, I Am...

APRIL 10

I AM HIS CHILD

CURTIS

"See what great love the Father has lavished on us, that we should be called children of God! And that is what we are! The reason the world does not know us is that it did not know Him" (1 John 3:1).

Today I Am His child.

HOW ABOUT YOU?

Today, I Am...

APRIL 11

I AM CAREFREE

ETHAN

The Bible says: "Cast all your cares upon Him because He cares for you" (1 Peter 5:7).

So I Am carefree today. Therefore, none of my choices today will give value to concerns because they are not real. I will operate in truth and freedom today. I say it again, I Am carefree.

HOW ABOUT YOU?

Today, I Am...

APRIL 12

I AM A REVEALER

TONY

A glorious morning to you, men. I observed something great in Scripture today: "He revealed His character to Moses and His deeds to the people of Israel" (1 Peter 5:7).

An entire people saw the deeds of God because of one man's relationship with God. It was through one man that God was revealed to an entire nation. That can be you and me. I want to be someone that has such relationship with God that many will see His deeds and be blessed through it ... a whole nation.

Today, I Am a revealer.

HOW ABOUT YOU?

Today, I Am...

APRIL 13

I AM GRATITUDE AND FAITH, RICHLY SATISFIED

TONY

2 Samuel 4:9 was my reading today; I love the little comment inserted by David: "As the Lord lives, who has redeemed my life out of every adversity."

I love that. I share that same thought. He has never failed me. Today, I Am gratitude and faith. A double shot of I am.

Bless you both.

ETHAN

Psalms 104 is all about acknowledging God for his power and creation, stretching out the starry curtain of the heavens. Verse 28 returns me to a favorite of mine, talking about all of creation.

"You open your hand to feed them, and they are richly satisfied."

That's me. I Am richly satisfied. I'm in want of nothing. In that sense, I come alongside Tony's gratitude. His provision for me is all that I want or need. I Am richly satisfied. I receive His abundance, knowing that it is unlimited, and that He's a good Father.

I Am satisfied ... richly!

HOW ABOUT YOU?

Today, I Am...

APRIL 14

I AM FEARLESS LOVE

CURTIS

> "There is no fear in love. But perfect love drives out fear, because fear has to do with punishment. The one who fears is not made perfect in love." (1 John 4:18).
>
> Today I Am fearless love and I share it with everyone around me.
>
> Blessings for today!

TONY

> Love it, Curtis. You ARE fearless love. Unleash it today, brother!

HOW ABOUT YOU?

> Today, I Am...

APRIL 15

I AM THANKS

ETHAN

"I give you thanks O Lord with my whole heart" (Psalms 138:1).

I Am thanks today, all day. And I love how David ends chapter 138 by saying, "The Lord will fulfill his purpose for me."

I know He will!

Bless you guys.

HOW ABOUT YOU?

Today, I Am...

APRIL 16

I AM SHINING

CURTIS

"Because of the tender mercy of our God, by which the rising sun will come to us from heaven to shine on those living in darkness and in the shadow of death, to guide our feet into the path of peace" (Luke 1:78-79).

May God's tender mercy be upon you both. May His light shine through you to bring the love of Jesus to everyone you know.

Today I Am shining, an instrument spreading God's love all around me to everyone I encounter. I will send love to all those who pass by and may even my shadow bless those around me.

HOW ABOUT YOU?

Today, I Am...

APRIL 17

I AM PURE

ETHAN

Today I share the well-known verse in Matthew about not swearing, but simply saying yes or no (I love the message translation!).

"You don't make your words true by embellishing them with religious lace. In making your speech sound more religious, it becomes less true. Just say 'yes' or 'no.' When you manipulate words to get your own way, you go wrong" (Matthew 5:34-37).

Today, I Am pure. There is nothing in me, or coming out of me, that is not of Him.

TONY

Awesome Ethan. I love pure! Nothing else needs to be added. You ARE pure, all day!

HOW ABOUT YOU?

Today, I Am...

APRIL 18

I AM ENTRUSTED, FIXED ON THE UNSEEN

TONY

> "As each has received a gift, use it to serve one another, as good stewards of God's varied grace" (1 Peter 4:10).
>
> All things are given us; His trust in us is limitless. He gives without exception and our will must be one with His in order to receive. His gifts are not for us alone, though; we must give to all we meet.
>
> Today, I Am entrusted.

CURTIS

> You are entrusted, Tony! Blessings surround you all day.
>
> "So we fix our eyes not on what is seen, but on what is unseen. For what is seen is temporary, but what is unseen is eternal" (2 Corinthians 4:18).
>
> Today, I Am fixed on the unseen, the eternal work of God in my life.

HOW ABOUT YOU?

> Today, I Am...

APRIL 19

I AM ANCHORED, GRACE

CURTIS

"We have this hope as an anchor for the soul, firm and secure. It enters the inner sanctuary behind the curtain" (Hebrews 6:19).

Today I Am anchored with hope, firm and secure. We are tethered to Jesus, and He holds us close!

TONY

Morning, men! Love anchored all day. You ARE!

John 1:16 says, "For from his fullness we have all received, grace upon grace."

I Am grace today. All day long!

CURTIS

You are grace upon grace, Tony!

HOW ABOUT YOU?

Today, I Am...

APRIL 20

I AM EYES ON HIM

ETHAN

2 Chronicles 20:12 is full of goodness, as Jehoshaphat prayed in preparation for battle. He started with this: "We do not know what to do, but our eyes are on you."

The rest is history. They were victorious and chapter 20 goes on to say that "they were three days in taking the spoil, it was so much" (2 Chronicles 20:25).

Interesting how it all started with one simple thought and prayer.

Today, I Am eyes on Him all day.

HOW ABOUT YOU?

Today, I Am...

APRIL 21

I AM UNSHAKEN

CURTIS

Jesus is the cornerstone.

Psalms 118:22 says, "The stone that the builders rejected has now become the cornerstone."

And in Isaiah 28:16, the Lord says, "'Look, I am placing a foundation stone in Jerusalem, a form and tested stone. It is a precious stone that is safe to build on. Whoever believes need never be shaken.'"

I Am unshaken! My belief is in Jesus as the true, safe-tested rock. The enemy has been defeated, and death couldn't hold Jesus down.

HOW ABOUT YOU?

Today, I Am...

APRIL 22

I AM SINGING FOR JOY

CURTIS

"Come, let us sing for joy to the Lord; let us shout aloud to the Rock of our salvation. Let us come before him with thanksgiving and extol him with music and song" (Psalms 95:1-2).

Today I Am singing for joy all day long!

God is surely with us, so we have much to sing about!

HOW ABOUT YOU?

Today, I Am...

APRIL 23

I AM PROTECTED

ETHAN

> In Micah 7:14-15, the people ask the Lord to protect them "as He did long ago," and God replies, "Yes, I will do mighty miracles for you, like those I did when I rescued you from slavery in Egypt."
>
> That's who He is—a God who says 'yes' to protection, 'yes' to rescue, and 'yes' to miracles.
>
> Today, I Am protected by the author and creator of all miracles; the one who holds all our prayers together!

TONY

> Yes, you ARE protected all day. I love it. He holds all things together.

HOW ABOUT YOU?

> Today, I Am...

APRIL 24

I AM SEPARATED WITH HIM
ETHAN

> I've been meditating on Matthew 6:6: "But when you pray, go into a private room and, closing the door, pray to your Father, Who is in secret."
>
> It's so important that we go to a secret place, away from the world. You'll recall when Noah built the ark, God shut the door. He shares His secrets with only those who go through the door, into the tent of meetings, seeking Him alone.
>
> I Am separated with Him and, therefore, accessing ancient secrets from (and with) Him. Loving you.

CURTIS

> Very powerful, Ethan. Love it and love the word you shared. Go through that door today and access all He has for you.

HOW ABOUT YOU?

> Today, I Am...

APRIL 25

I AM REDEEMED

CURTIS

> "But now, this is what the Lord says— he who created you, O Jacob, he who formed you, O Israel: 'Fear not, for I have redeemed you; I have summoned you by name; you are mine'" (Isaiah 43:1).
>
> Today I Am redeemed, forgiven and made new for His perfect plan.
>
> Blessings for an amazing week!

HOW ABOUT YOU?

Today, I Am...

APRIL 26

I AM ABUNDANCE

TONY

> Jesus says, "I came that they may have life and have it abundantly" (John 10:10).
>
> I Am abundance today, moment by moment, all day long. Nothing but abundance.

ETHAN

> Have an abundant day full of good works and great blessings!

HOW ABOUT YOU?

> Today, I Am...

APRIL 27

I AM A WRESTLER WITH GOD
ETHAN

"The man said, 'But no longer. Your name is no longer Jacob. From now on it's Israel (God-Wrestler); you've wrestled with God and you've come through'" (Genesis 32:28).

Today I Am a wrestler with God, using His blessing to be a blessing to all around me!

HOW ABOUT YOU?

Today, I Am...

APRIL 28

I AM PEACE

TONY

"Now may the Lord of peace himself give you peace at all times and in every way. The Lord be with all of you" (2 Thessalonians 3:16).

Today, I Am peace at all times and in every way!

HOW ABOUT YOU?

Today, I Am...

APRIL 29

I AM RICHLY SATISFIED

ETHAN

"No one can serve two masters ... You cannot serve both God and money" (Matthew 6:24).

Money has no grip on me—none! I Am richly satisfied. The Lord has me right where he wants me. The desires of my heart are for Him and His plans to manifest in and through me. I celebrate the freedom from money that comes from Christ! Thank you, God!

HOW ABOUT YOU?

Today, I Am...

APRIL 30

I AM OVERFLOWING

CURTIS

"So then, just as you received Christ Jesus as Lord, continue to live in Him, rooted and built up in Him, strengthened in the faith as you were taught, and overflowing with thankfulness" (Colossians 2:6-7).

Today, I Am overflowing with thankfulness all day long!

HOW ABOUT YOU?

Today, I Am...

MAY 1

I AM STRONG WITH HIS MIGHT
TONY

"Be strong in the Lord and in the strength of His might" (Ephesians 6:10).

Makes me think of power, His power. Today I Am strong with His might, all day long, and I claim all good that He has in store for us today and that we be strong ambassadors for Him all day.

HOW ABOUT YOU?

Today, I Am...

MAY 2

I AM EXALTED IN UNION
CURTIS

"Be still and know that I am God; I will be exalted among the nations, I will be exalted in the earth" (Psalms 46:10).

Today, I Am exalted in union with my Heavenly Father.

HOW ABOUT YOU?

Today, I Am...

MAY 3

I AM IN THE LIGHT OF HIS UNFAILING LOVE

ETHAN

Good morning. In Psalms 25:7, David says, "Do not remember the rebellious sins of my youth [but] remember me in the light of your unfailing love."

Love this! Today, I Am in the light of his unfailing love. Loving you today (from inside His light).

CURTIS

Ethan, you always shine that light!

HOW ABOUT YOU?

Today, I Am...

MAY 4

I AM CONFIDENT IN THE LORD
CURTIS

"Lean on, trust in, and be confident in the Lord with all your heart and mind and do not rely on your own insight or understanding" (Proverbs 3:5).

Today I Am confident in the Lord, not relying on my understanding but wholly trusting in Him.

Blessings, my brothers!

HOW ABOUT YOU?

Today, I Am...

MAY 5

I AM FREE

ETHAN

> "Do not judge others and you will not be judged. For you will be treated as you treat others" (Matthew 7:1-2).
>
> I Am free. I judge no one, and no one is my judge (only God). I see only the light in people. It surrounds me.

CURTIS

> You ARE free, and I see your light brightly shining.

HOW ABOUT YOU?

> Today, I Am...

MAY 6

I AM TRUSTING

TONY

> I love you guys, and your faith and strength give me faith and strength. Today I read about Jesus in the wilderness in John 4, combating the devil. The two verses that stuck out to me were the first—"Jesus was led by the Spirit into the wilderness"—and the last, verse 11—"Then the devil went away, and angels came and took care of Jesus."
>
> It reminds me that God goes before us and leads us; God cares about us and sends us helpers and angels.
>
> Thank you, God! Jesus' reaction was simple trust.
>
> Today, I Am trusting, like Jesus. Wherever He leads, I will go, and be cared for!

HOW ABOUT YOU?

Today, I Am...

MAY 7

I AM COMPLETELY CARED FOR BY GOD

ETHAN

> Genesis 8:1 exemplifies God's care for us and omnipotence in every aspect of the world: "But God remembered Noah and all the wild animals and the livestock that were with him in the ark, and he sent a wind over the earth, and the waters receded.
>
> I Am completely cared for by God.

HOW ABOUT YOU?

Today, I Am...

MAY 8

I AM FERTILE SOIL

ETHAN

> I can feel powerful things happening in my life. I feel that mighty winds are behind me; God is propelling me His way. My heart is full of praise and gratitude.
>
> "Still other seeds fell on fertile soil, and they produced a crop that was thirty, sixty, and even a hundred times as much as had been planted!" (Matthew 13:8).
>
> I Am fertile soil. I receive the seed, and exponential growth is being produced all around me.

CURTIS

> You ARE fertile soil and God is bringing forth a mighty harvest!

HOW ABOUT YOU?

Today, I Am...

MAY 9

I AM RUNNING WITH JESUS
TONY

"Therefore, since we are surrounded by such a great cloud of witnesses, let us throw off everything that hinders and the sin that so easily entangles. And let us run with perseverance the race marked out for us, fixing our eyes on Jesus, the pioneer and perfecter of faith. For the joy set before him he endured the cross, scorning its shame, and sat down at the right hand of the throne of God" (Hebrews 12:1-2).

Today I Am running with Jesus, the perfecter of my faith.

HOW ABOUT YOU?

Today, I Am...

MAY 10

I AM KNOWN

CURTIS

"O Lord, you have searched me and you know me. You know when I sit and when I rise; you perceive my thoughts from afar. You discern my going out and my lying down; you are familiar with all my ways. Before a word is on my tongue you know it completely, O Lord" (Psalms 139:1-4).

Today I Am known, and I have nothing to hide. My Father's love is complete and my goal is to share His love.

TONY

Awesome, Curtis. What a great morning already with the powerful words exchanged. Look out week/world; here we come!

HOW ABOUT YOU?

Today, I Am...

MAY 11

I AM TRANSFORMING

ETHAN

"The Kingdom of God is like a mustard seed planted in a field. It is the smallest of all seeds, but becomes ... a tree" (Matthew 13:31-32).

I Am transforming. I am going from seed to tree as a businessman, as a husband, as a father. I am going from seed to tree as a believer and child of God. And my knowledge, my relationships, my ability to love and forgive, and even my bank accounts, will manifest that I Am transforming.

CURTIS

I love transforming; it is growth, constant, awesome. You ARE transforming all day, from seed to tree.

HOW ABOUT YOU?

Today, I Am...

MAY 12

I AM JOYFUL IN GOD MY SAVIOR
CURTIS

> Here's to this week, prayed over with our Father's favor: "Though the fig tree does not bud and there are no grapes on the vines, though the olive crop fails and the fields produce no food, though there are no sheep in the pen and no cattle in the stalls, yet I will rejoice in the Lord, I will be joyful in God my Savior. The Sovereign Lord is my strength; He makes my feet like the feet of a deer, He enables me to go on the heights" (Habakkuk 3:17-19).
>
> Today I Am joyful in God my Savior all day long!

HOW ABOUT YOU?

Today, I Am...

MAY 13

I AM TRUTH

TONY

> Mighty men, the Beatitudes open with "God blesses those who are poor and realize their need for Him, for the Kingdom of Heaven is theirs" (Matthew 5:3).
>
> Today, I Am truth—the truth that I need God and nothing else. And I will live that truth all day long, giving value to nothing else but God.

HOW ABOUT YOU?

> Today, I Am...

MAY 14

I AM RESTING

CURTIS

"He who dwells in the shelter of the Most High will rest in the shadow of the Almighty" (Psalms 91:1).

Today I Am resting in the Almighty, as His strength is made perfect in my weakness.

"...but He said to me, 'My grace is sufficient for you, for power is made perfect in weakness.' So, I will boast all the more gladly of my weaknesses, so that the power of Christ may dwell in me" (2 Corinthians 12:9).

HOW ABOUT YOU?

Today, I Am...

MAY 15

I AM TRUSTING HIM

ETHAN

"Give God the right to direct your life, and as you trust him along the way you'll find he pulled it off perfectly!" (Psalms 37:5).

This is me today! I Am trusting Him.

HOW ABOUT YOU?

Today, I Am...

MAY 16

I AM PEACE WITH JESUS

CURTIS

"While they were still talking about this, Jesus himself stood among them and said to them, 'Peace be with you'" (Luke 24:36).

I Am peace with Jesus! I love who you both are!

HOW ABOUT YOU?

Today, I Am...

MAY 17

I AM BOLDNESS OF FAITH

ETHAN

Today, Peter's most amazing statement exclaims, "Lord, if it's really you, tell me to come to you, walking on the water" (Matthew 14:28). Peter had the boldness of faith to get out of the boat. Today, I Am boldness of faith. I see no limitations, only God's power and goodness.

HOW ABOUT YOU?

Today, I Am...

MAY 18

I AM FAVOR

TONY

> I love this promise from Psalms 84:11: "The Lord bestows favor and honor."
>
> I accept it today and I Am favor all day.
>
> Bless you both!

CURTIS

> Blessings to you and your family, Tony. His favor is all over you!

HOW ABOUT YOU?

Today, I Am...

MAY 19

I AM BELIEF

ETHAN

"And so He did only a few miracles there because of their unbelief" (Matthew 13:58).

The people got what they expected. I Am belief. I believe in miracles. I call down all the miracles of heaven into my life; I claim that miracles will happen daily to me and through me.

HOW ABOUT YOU?

Today, I Am...

MAY 20

I AM KNOCKING

CURTIS

"Ask and it will be given to you; seek and you will find; knock and the door will be opened to you" (Matthew 7:7).

I Am knocking and expectantly excited for what God has in store for us today!

TONY

Hallelujah, my brother. You are a-knockin'.

HOW ABOUT YOU?

Today, I Am...

MAY 21

I AM LIVING BY FAITH

ETHAN

"We live by faith, not by sight" (2 Corinthians 5:7).

Today I Am living by faith. Blessings come to those who look forward with faith!

HOW ABOUT YOU?

Today, I Am...

MAY 22

I AM FOUGHT FOR

ETHAN

> Joshua spoke his final encouragement: "God has driven out superpower nations before you. And up to now, no one has been able to stand up to you. Think of it—one of you, single-handedly, putting a thousand on the run! Because God is God, your God. Because He fights for you, just as He promised you" (Joshua 23:9-10).
>
> Today I Am fought for all day long!

HOW ABOUT YOU?

> Today, I Am...

MAY 23

I AM ALL IN

TONY

> Isaiah 54:2 says, "Enlarge the place of your tent, and let the curtains of your habitations be stretched out ... do not hold back."
>
> My prayer for us today is we don't limit the unlimited. May He give us the capacity to receive all He has for us and help us to have the capacity to give all we have to others.
>
> Today, I will not hold back, so therefore I Am all in, all day!

HOW ABOUT YOU?

Today, I Am...

MAY 24

I AM FREE OF ME

ETHAN

Jesus said, "If you try to hang on to your life, you will lose it. But if you give up your life for my sake, you will save it" (Matthew 16:25).

I Am free of me. I no longer live, but Christ lives in me. The exchanged life is the only life. I celebrate it today and I claim it for myself.

Blessings for your day.

HOW ABOUT YOU?

Today, I Am...

MAY 25

I AM FRUIT-FILLED

CURTIS

> "But the fruit of the Spirit is love, joy, peace, patience, kindness, goodness, faithfulness, gentleness and self-control. Against such things there is no law" (Galatians 5:22-23).
>
> Today I Am fruit-filled by the Spirit, all day long!

HOW ABOUT YOU?

Today, I Am...

MAY 26

I AM FAITH

ETHAN

Today I re-read Matthew 17:20, when Jesus says, "If you have faith as small as a mustard seed ... Nothing would be impossible."

Nothing means nothing. I Am faith. So all things are possible. Loving you guys.

HOW ABOUT YOU?

Today, I Am...

MAY 27

I AM LOVED AND LOVING THOSE AROUND ME

CURTIS

"The Lord appeared to us in the past, saying:
'I have loved you with an everlasting love;
I have drawn you with loving-kindness'" (Jeremiah 31:3).

Today I Am loved and loving those around me (like you!) with His everlasting love!

HOW ABOUT YOU?

Today, I Am...

MAY 28

I AM COURAGE

TONY

The Bible says Ezra had set his heart to study the Law of the Lord and to teach these laws in Israel. In Ezra 7:6, the Bible states two times that "the hand of The Lord his God was on him."

I love what Ezra wrote in verses 27 and 28: "Blessed be the Lord ... who extended to me his steadfast love ... I took courage, for the hand of the Lord my God was on me."

Others knew, Ezra knew, the hand of the Lord was on him.

Today, the hand of the Lord is on us. Let us have courage as Ezra did. I Am courage, all day.

HOW ABOUT YOU?

Today, I Am...

MAY 29

I AM JUSTIFIED FREELY

ETHAN

I am "justified freely through the redemption that came from Jesus Christ" (Romans 3:24).

So I Am justified freely. Thank you, Jesus!

HOW ABOUT YOU?

Today, I Am...

MAY 30

I AM DELIVERED, SURROUNDED

CURTIS

"You are my hiding place;
you will protect me from trouble
and surround me with songs of deliverance" (Psalms 32:7).

Today, I Am delivered from all fear, anxiety, loneliness and despair. I Am surrounded by His love and protection.

ETHAN

Curtis, you ARE delivered, and you ARE surrounded. That's a double-shot of truth.

HOW ABOUT YOU?

Today, I Am...

MAY 31

I AM FEARLESS, STEADFASTLY TRUSTING

ETHAN

"He has no fear of bad news whose heart is steadfast trusting in the Lord" (Psalms 112:7).

That verse is for you today, and for me. Today, I Am fearless, steadfastly trusting.

HOW ABOUT YOU?

Today, I Am...

JUNE 1

I AM EMPOWERED BY THE SPIRIT OF THE LORD

CURTIS

> God's work through Samson's life is really incredible: "As [Samson] approached Lehi, the Philistines came toward him shouting. The Spirit of the Lord came powerfully upon him. The ropes on his arms became like charred flax, and the bindings dropped from his hands" (Judges 15:14).
>
> I Am empowered by the spirit of our Lord!

HOW ABOUT YOU?

Today, I Am...

JUNE 2

I AM BLESSING THE LORD

TONY

> I take my I Am today from a simple well-known verse, Psalms 103: "Bless the Lord, O my soul, and all that is within me."
>
> I Am blessing the Lord today, all day long—just Him, nothing else.

HOW ABOUT YOU?

> Today, I Am...

JUNE 3

I AM UTTERLY DEVOTED TO JESUS

CURTIS

I love the devotion here in Ruth 1:16: "But Ruth replied, 'Don't urge me to leave you or to turn back from you. Where you go I will go, and where you stay I will stay. Your people will be my people and your God my God.'"

I Am utterly devoted to Jesus.

HOW ABOUT YOU?

Today, I Am...

JUNE 4

I AM STRENGTHENED

ETHAN

Here's a great verse that's been cited before, but not in some time: "The eyes of the Lord search the whole earth looking to strengthen those whose hearts are fully committed to Him" (2 Chronicles 16:9).

Love you guys. I Am strengthened, thanks to you!

HOW ABOUT YOU?

Today, I Am...

JUNE 5

I AM ENCIRCLED

CURTIS

"Benjamin: 'God's beloved; God's permanent residence. Encircled by God all day long, within whom God is at home.'" (Deuteronomy 33:12)

Today I Am encircled by God all day long!

ETHAN

Love it, Curtis. You ARE encircled by God. That's the truth. I claim it for myself and Tony today, too.

HOW ABOUT YOU?

Today, I Am...

JUNE 6

I AM QUIET

ETHAN

"Better to have one handful with quietness than two handfuls with hard work and chasing the wind" (Ecclesiastes 4:6).

If we have more riches and more noise in our lives, we are no closer to God. But if we have quiet, we can then hear the still, small voice of God. Then we will go as He directs, and not chase the wind.

I Am quiet today.

HOW ABOUT YOU?

Today, I Am...

JUNE 7

I AM ABLAZE

TONY

My brothers! We all may know the Lord's Prayer, but I was blessed to read it in The Message this morning, quite different sounding, and wonderful, so I share it with you here.

"Our Father in heaven, reveal who you are. Set the world right; do what's best—as above, so below. Keep us alive with three square meals. Keep us forgiven with you and forgiving others. Keep us safe from ourselves and the devil. You're in charge! You can do anything you want! You're ablaze in beauty! Yes. Yes. Yes."

Today, I Am ablaze!

HOW ABOUT YOU?

Today, I Am...

JUNE 8

I AM SUPERNATURAL STRENGTH
CURTIS

"But God faced him directly: 'Go in this strength that is yours. Save Israel from Midian. Haven't I just sent you?'" (Judges 6:14).

Today I Am supernatural strength, going as God has sent me!

HOW ABOUT YOU?

Today, I Am...

JUNE 9

I AM AMIDST GOD

ETHAN

> Happy Friday, brothers. Today, I think of you both when I read in Matthew 18:19-20, "If two of you agree here on earth concerning anything you ask, my Father in heaven will do it for you. For where two or three gather together as my followers, I am there among them."
>
> This is for us! We gather together every morning, and God is with us. Today, I Am amidst God, who is for me.

HOW ABOUT YOU?

> Today, I Am…

JUNE 10

I AM RUNNING WITH PERSEVERANCE

CURTIS

"Therefore, since we are surrounded by such a great cloud of witnesses, let us throw off everything that hinders and the sin that so easily entangles, and let us run with perseverance the race marked out for us. Let us fix our eyes on Jesus, the author and perfecter of our faith, who for the joy set before him endured the cross, scorning its shame, and sat down at the right hand of the throne of God" (Hebrews 12:1-2).

Today I Am running with perseverance, all day long!

TONY

I love Hebrews 12, and you ARE running with perseverance all day, brother!

HOW ABOUT YOU?

Today, I Am...

JUNE 11

I AM FORGIVENESS UNENDING
ETHAN

> Good morning, men. It's a great day to love the world! Peter asked how many times he must forgive a brother who sins against him; up to seven times? Jesus answered, "I tell you, not seven times, but seventy-seven times" (Matthew 18:22).
>
> There is no end to God's forgiveness, and there is no end to mine. I Am forgiveness unending. And that frees me up to love unhindered.

CURTIS

> Thanks for sharing, brother. Love it! You ARE forgiveness unending; I have experienced it myself.

HOW ABOUT YOU?

Today, I Am...

JUNE 12

I AM PEACE AND HOLINESS
TONY

"Strive for peace with everyone, and for the holiness without which no one will see the Lord" (Hebrews 12:14).

I Am peace and holiness today. Double shot!

HOW ABOUT YOU?

Today, I Am...

JUNE 13

I AM HIS LOVE IN FULL EXPRESSION

ETHAN

"If we love each other, God lives in us, and His love is brought to full expression in us" (1 John 4:12).

I Am His love in full expression. That's who I Am. And I love both of you, and I am praying for everyone for victory today.

HOW ABOUT YOU?

Today, I Am...

JUNE 14

I AM SHINED UPON

TONY

"Many are asking, 'Who can show us any good?' Let the light of your face shine upon us, O Lord. You have filled my heart with greater joy than when their grain and new wine abound. I will lie down and sleep in peace, for you alone, O Lord, make me dwell in safety" (Psalms 4:6-8).

Today I Am shined upon, my heart is filled with great joy all day long.

HOW ABOUT YOU?

Today, I Am...

JUNE 15

I AM LOVE, HIS CHILD, I KNOW GOD

ETHAN

> I look forward to the blessings of fellowship with you this morning. The Bible shows good things happen at mountain tops! Today I read this from 1 John 4:7: "Anyone who loves is a child of God and knows God."
>
> I Am love, I Am His child, and I KNOW God. A holy hat-trick.

CURTIS

> Thanks for getting the week started right, Ethan!

HOW ABOUT YOU?

Today, I Am...

JUNE 16

YOU ARE LIGHT

TONY

> Men, happy day to you. I read Matthew 5:16 and was reminded of who you both are.
>
> "Let your light shine before others, so that they may see your good works and give glory to your Father who is in heaven."
>
> You ARE light to me and many, many others every day. I am thankful for you both.

CURTIS

> Thanks, Tony. Your light shines brightly in our lives.

ETHAN

> Thank you, Tony. One of my favorite verses, and you personify it.

HOW ABOUT YOU?

> Today, I Am...

JUNE 17

I AM LISTENING TO JESUS

CURTIS

> I've always loved the Transfiguration. It seems so pregnant with meaning.
>
> From the mouth of God: "This is my dearly loved Son, who brings me joy. Listen to him" (Matthew 17:5).
>
> That simple statement shifts our focus from the law (stone tablets of the first mount) to the life of Jesus; in comes the New Testament. Today, I'm doing just what my Father says: I Am listening to Jesus, all day long.

ETHAN

> Love is the way!

HOW ABOUT YOU?

> Today, I Am...

JUNE 18

I AM HIS WILL

TONY

"But as for me, my prayer is to you, O Lord. At an acceptable time, O God, in the abundance of your steadfast love answer me in your saving faithfulness" (Psalms 69:13).

This calls for patience and a faith knowing He will answer, as well as acknowledging His will, His way.

Today I Am His will all day.

CURTIS

Beautiful, Tony. You ARE His will. I am praying for you both and believe He is going to do big things now, this week. Can't wait to see what manifests from our faithful prayers this week. He is so good.

HOW ABOUT YOU?

Today, I Am...

JUNE 19

I AM EARNESTLY SEEKING OUR LORD

CURTIS

"And without faith it is impossible to please God, because anyone who comes to him must believe that he exists and that he rewards those who earnestly seek him"
(Hebrews 11:6).

Today I Am earnestly seeking our Lord with faith for His pleasure, all day long.

HOW ABOUT YOU?

Today, I Am...

JUNE 20

I AM FREE, SELF-SUFFICIENT IN CHRIST'S SUFFICIENCY

ETHAN

> Good morning, gentlemen. I Am free today. "God sent him to buy freedom for us who were slaves to the law " (Galatians 4:5).
>
> "He sets the prisoners free and gives them joy" (Psalms 68:6).
>
> Whom the Son set free is free indeed! And that's me. All day long.

CURTIS

> "I have strength for all things in Christ who empowers me. [I am ready for anything and equal to anything through Him who infuses inner strength into me; I am self-sufficient in Christ's sufficiency]" (Philippians 4:13).
>
> I Am self-sufficient in Christ's sufficiency, all day long!

HOW ABOUT YOU?

Today, I Am...

JUNE 21

I AM HANDPICKED BY GOD
CURTIS

"Even as he chose us in Him before the foundation of the world, that we should be holy and blameless before Him. In love He predestined us for adoption as sons through Jesus Christ" (Ephesians 1:4-5).

There is a lot of good in these two verses! We were chosen before the world was created. Today, I Am handpicked by God. And I am extending His love to all those around me.

HOW ABOUT YOU?

Today, I Am...

JUNE 22

I AM FORGIVEN

ETHAN

In Mark 2, they lowered the paralyzed man down through the roof and, in verse 5, Jesus says, "Your sins are forgiven."

But there was a disconnect. The crowd wanted to see a physical healing, and He was giving spiritual healing. Jesus placed far more importance on spiritual health than physical health, forgiveness over wellness. The ultimate proof of this was His physical suffering for our forgiveness.

So, today, I Am forgiven. The miracle of that forgiveness has no end, and I receive (and need) it all.

HOW ABOUT YOU?

Today, I Am...

JUNE 23

I AM FIRSTLY HIS

TONY

> Matthew 6:33 says it all: "Seek first His kingdom and His righteousness, and all these things will be given you to you as well."
>
> Today, I Am firstly His. I believe no lies about the importance of anything else. I will be able to bring love and light to this world.

CURTIS

> Yes, you ARE firstly His! All day long!

HOW ABOUT YOU?

> Today, I Am...

JUNE 24

I AM GOD'S AND GOD'S ALONE
ETHAN

> The book of 1 John closes with this final line: "Dear Children, keep away from anything that might take God's place in your hearts" (1 John 5:21)
>
> My heart is His place. The world has lost its lure. I Am God's and God's alone.

HOW ABOUT YOU?

> Today, I Am...

JUNE 25

I AM KNOWING GOD MORE AND MORE

ETHAN

> Jesus said to the woman at the well, "If you knew who I was, you'd be asking me for a drink" (John 4:10).
>
> Knowing God is the key to everything. I Am knowing God more and more. The more I know Him, the more freely I live.

HOW ABOUT YOU?

Today, I Am…

JUNE 26

I AM ABOUNDING IN THANKSGIVING

TONY

"So walk in him, rooted and built up in him and established in the faith ... abounding in thanksgiving" (Colossians 2:6-7).

I Am abounding in thanksgiving today as I walk in HIM.

HOW ABOUT YOU?

Today, I Am...

JUNE 27

I AM PERSEVERANCE

CURTIS

I'm following along in James ...

"Perseverance must finish its work so that you may be mature and complete, not lacking anything" (James 1:4).

Today I Am perseverance, all day long.

HOW ABOUT YOU?

Today, I Am...

JUNE 28

I AM FOLLOWING JESUS

CURTIS

"Whoever serves me must follow me; and where I am, my servant also will be. My Father will honor the one who serves me" (John 12:26).

Today I Am following Jesus. We are right here together!

HOW ABOUT YOU?

Today, I Am...

JUNE 29

I AM BEARING FRUIT

TONY

> I am going to borrow one small verse today from Colossians 1:10: "Bearing fruit in every good work."
>
> I Am bearing fruit today, in every good work, all day long.
>
> Bless you both!

HOW ABOUT YOU?

Today, I Am...

JUNE 30

I AM STILL

CURTIS

> "Be still, and know that I am God;
> I will be exalted among the nations,
> I will be exalted in the earth" (Psalms 46:10).
>
> Today I Am still, for I know our Father has great plans for us today.

HOW ABOUT YOU?

Today, I Am...

JULY 1

I AM SECURE IN HIM

ETHAN

> Today, I read a description of the Son of Man in Revelation 1:15. It's amazing. We have so much in store for us when we see Him for ourselves. There's so much there, but I like this nugget: "His feet were like polished bronze refined in a furnace."
>
> I tell you this morning, Jesus is sturdy, steady, and stable. All His trials have served only to polish his feet. He is a strong foundation. So today, I Am secure in Him. I can lean on His strength. Thank you, Jesus!

HOW ABOUT YOU?

> Today, I Am...

JULY 2

I AM HOLDING FAST MY RIGHTEOUSNESS

TONY

Reading Job the past few days as part of my thematic reading this year. Difficult book to read, except I know how it ends, which makes it much easier. Sometimes our days are difficult, or periods of our life are difficult. My prayer is that this book in the Bible may serve as a reminder to me that I know how it ends. And knowing the end makes all seem much less challenging. We have a great ending, a promise, and a great story to share, so may I be like Job when he says "As long as my breath is in me, and the spirit of God is in my nostrils ... till I die I will not put away my integrity from me. I hold fast my righteousness and will not let it go" (Job 27:3-6).

I Am holding fast my righteousness all day long!

HOW ABOUT YOU?

Today, I Am...

JULY 3

I AM GUIDED BY GOD TO A GLORIOUS DESTINY

ETHAN

> This year has been great, and what we continue to create this year will be magnificent. Psalms 73:24 says,
>
> "You guide me with your counsel, leading me to a glorious destiny" (Psalms 73:24).
>
> I Am guided by God to a glorious destiny.
>
> Amen!

HOW ABOUT YOU?

Today, I Am...

JULY 4

I AM A DIFFERENT SPIRIT, CLINGING TO JESUS

TONY

I love what the Lord said about Caleb in Numbers 14:23-24: "And none of those who despised me shall see it but my servant Caleb, because he has a different spirit and has followed me fully."

I Am a different spirit today, following Him fully, all day long.

Bless you both. I prayed powerful favor over you this morning.

CURTIS

I receive His powerful favor and I thank you for mustering His Heavenly forces to deliver it!

"Because you are my help,
I sing in the shadow of your wings.
My soul clings to you;
your right hand upholds me" (Psalms 63:7-8).

I Am clinging to Jesus all day long, held tightly in return under the shadow of His wings ... all day long!

HOW ABOUT YOU?

Today, I Am...

JULY 5

I AM FOLLOWING IN HIS STEPS

CURTIS

"To this you were called, because Christ suffered for you, leaving you an example, that you should follow in his steps" (1 Peter 2:21).

Today I Am following in His steps, all day long.

HOW ABOUT YOU?

Today, I Am...

JULY 6

I AM LISTENING PEACEFULLY

ETHAN

> Today I quote James 1:19: "Be quick to listen, slow to speak and slow to anger."
>
> I Am listening peacefully today.

HOW ABOUT YOU?

> Today, I Am...

JULY 7

I AM THANKS

TONY

> "And they were to stand every morning, thanking and praising the Lord, and likewise at evening" (1 Chronicles 23:30).
>
> I Am thanks to Him, all day long.
>
> Love you guys; blessings, my dear brothers!

HOW ABOUT YOU?

Today, I Am...

JULY 8

I AM LOOKING TO OUR LORD

CURTIS

"Look to the Lord and his strength; seek his face always" (Psalms 105:4).

Today I Am looking to our Lord and receiving His strength!

HOW ABOUT YOU?

Today, I Am...

JULY 9

I AM CELEBRATING LIFE ETERNAL

ETHAN

> "Blessed are those who are invited to the wedding feast of the Lamb" (Revelation 19:9).
>
> There's an invitation with my name on it! Today, I Am celebrating life eternal. I give my life over to God anew, ask for a fresh anointing of the Spirit, and move in the blessing of the wedding feast that is to come.

CURTIS

> Ethan, you ARE celebrating life eternal. That is who you ARE every day.

HOW ABOUT YOU?

Today, I Am...

JULY 10

I AM LISTENING TO HIS VOICE

CURTIS

"Whether you turn to the right or to the left, your ears will hear a voice behind you, saying, 'This is the way; walk in it'" (Isaiah 30:21).

Today I Am listening to His voice all day long!

HOW ABOUT YOU?

Today, I Am...

JULY 11

I AM LIGHT

ETHAN

> Revelation 21:23 describes heaven and it is breathtaking. I am so excited to see it! Here is a nugget: "And the city has no need of sun or moon, for the glory of God illuminates the city, and the Lamb is its light."
>
> I Am light, and I will shine for the glory of God today. Let me know how I can be a light to you today.

HOW ABOUT YOU?

> Today, I Am...

JULY 12

I AM ONE WITH GOD ALMIGHTY

TONY

> King Jehoshaphat hears that Judah is about to be attacked, so he assembles everyone at the temple and says, "If calamity comes upon us ... we will stand in your presence before this temple that bears your Name and will cry out to you in our distress, and you will hear us and save us'" (2 Chronicles 20:9).
>
> I love how confident the last phrase is. Victory comes from relationship, so I Am one with God almighty.

HOW ABOUT YOU?

> Today, I Am...

JULY 13

I AM GIVEN A GOD-LISTENING HEART

CURTIS

> "Here's what I want: Give me a God-listening heart so I can lead your people well, discerning the difference between good and evil" (1 Kings 3:9).
>
> Today I Am given a God-listening heart. And I act with His wisdom.

HOW ABOUT YOU?

> Today, I Am...

JULY 14

I AM DIFFERENT

ETHAN

"At that time the Spirit of the Lord will come powerfully upon you ... and you will be changed into a different person" (1 Samuel 10:6).

That's true of me! The Holy Spirit has come upon me, and I Am different. I celebrate being different. I am peculiar to the world, and even to my old self. Loving you both today.

HOW ABOUT YOU?

Today, I Am...

JULY 15

I AM STANDING FIRM

TONY

> I adopted Philippians 4 as my word of the week, and today I share verse 1: "Stand firm thus in the Lord."
>
> That is me, I Am standing firm in the Lord all day, moment by moment.

HOW ABOUT YOU?

Today, I Am...

JULY 16

I AM FOLLOWING THE PATH OF LIFE

CURTIS

"You will show me the path of life;
In Your presence is fullness of joy;
At Your right hand are pleasures forevermore" (Psalms 16:11).

Today, I Am following the path of life, experiencing the fullness of His joy.

Love you both!

HOW ABOUT YOU?

Today, I Am...

JULY 17

I AM ALONE WITH GOD

ETHAN

"Before daybreak the next morning, Jesus got up and went out to an isolated place to pray" (Mark 1:35).

Jesus needed alone time with his Father. It was a priority. Before daybreak, I was praying and then studying. Like Jesus, I Am alone with God. It's who I Am. And I love my relationship with my Father.

HOW ABOUT YOU?

Today, I Am...

JULY 18

I AM LOOKING TO JESUS

TONY

"Let us run with endurance the race that is set before us, looking to Jesus, the founder and perfecter of our faith" (Hebrews 12:1-2).

Eyes on the real prize: I Am looking to Jesus today, thanking Him for perfecting my faith.

HOW ABOUT YOU?

Today, I Am...

JULY 19

I AM STRUGGLING WITH ALL HIS ENERGY

CURTIS

"To this end I labor, struggling with all his energy, which so powerfully works in me" (Colossians 1:29).

Today I Am struggling with all His energy, expecting His powerful work to be made manifest in me.

HOW ABOUT YOU?

Today, I Am...

JULY 20

I AM TRANSFORMED BY A RENEWED MIND

ETHAN

> Today I go with a favorite verse: "Do not conform to the patterns of this world but be transformed by the renewing of your mind" (Romans 12:2).
>
> I Am transformed by a renewed mind. All day. Love you guys!

HOW ABOUT YOU?

Today, I Am...

JULY 21

I AM CHOSEN

CURTIS

"But you are a chosen people, a royal priesthood, a holy nation, a people belonging to God, that you may declare the praises of him who called you out of darkness into his wonderful light" (1 Peter 2:9).

Today I Am chosen and praising God all day long!

HOW ABOUT YOU?

Today, I Am...

JULY 22

I AM GENTLENESS

ETHAN

> I love James 3:13: "If you consider yourself to be wise ... [in] the ways of God, advertise it with a beautiful, fruitful life guided by wisdom's gentleness."
>
> Today I Am gentleness. Love you both this happy day.

CURTIS

> You are gentleness, and it is a blessed gift to all around you!

HOW ABOUT YOU?

Today, I Am...

JULY 23

I AM REJOICING

TONY

"This is the day that the Lord has made; let us rejoice and be glad in it" (Psalms 118:24).

I Am grateful for God's gift of today. I Am rejoicing all day long.

HOW ABOUT YOU?

Today, I Am...

JULY 24

I AM HUMBLE

CURTIS

"Humble yourselves, therefore, under God's mighty hand, that He may lift you up in due time" (1 Peter 5:6).

Today I Am humble, patiently waiting for Him to lift me up in due time.

HOW ABOUT YOU?

Today, I Am...

JULY 25

I AM ALIVE FOREVER AND EVER

ETHAN

> When John saw the vision of Jesus in Revelation 1:17-18 (eyes of fire, polished bronze feet), he fell at His feet as if dead. But the vision of Jesus laid his right hand on him and said, "Don't be afraid! I AM the First and the Last. I AM the living one. I died, but look—I AM alive forever and ever!"
>
> Here Jesus gives three identity statements of his own. I join Jesus and declare that I Am alive forever and ever. Hallelujah. Praise the one who paid my debts and raised this life up from the dead! Again I say I Am alive forever and ever!

TONY

> What a powerful I am, Ethan. Love that! And you ARE!

HOW ABOUT YOU?

> Today, I Am...

JULY 26

I AM PEACE

TONY

> Philippians 4:6 simply states, "Do not be anxious about anything."
>
> That leaves nothing out, nothing to be anxious about or worried about!
>
> I Am peace, all day.

CURTIS

> You ARE peace, Tony. It's supernatural how easy you roll through adversity. It's one of the biggest signs your faith is real and dynamic.

HOW ABOUT YOU?

> Today, I Am...

JULY 27

I AM NEW

ETHAN

"And the one sitting on the throne said, 'Look, I am making everything new!'" (Revelations 21:5).

I Am new. I let go of everything in my past so that I am completely free to serve my Father today. It's like I was born today. I have fresh eyes, fresh ears, fresh energy, fresh wisdom, new perspective. I cling to nothing of the past. I Am new, and ready to be who HE wants me to be today.

TONY

Ethan, you ARE new today, all day. I love that identity. It reminds me of a favorite phrase once shared with me: "Today I begin a new life."

Every day, new!

HOW ABOUT YOU?

Today, I Am...

JULY 28

I AM PRAISING AND THANKING HIM

TONY

Morning, mighty men! Thanks Ethan for your prayers. It reminds me of Psalms 136, the chapter has 26 verses with a praise or a thanks in each verse to God followed by "His steadfast love endures forever."

I Am praising and thanking Him today for His steadfast love. He never wavers and does wonders in my life day after day. Bless you both.

You ARE prayed for as well!

HOW ABOUT YOU?

Today, I Am...

JULY 29

I AM ETERNALLY BLESSED
CURTIS

> "Surely you have granted Him eternal blessings and made Him glad with the joy of your presence" (Psalms 21:6).
>
> Today I Am eternally blessed. God is filling us with the joy of His presence, ALL DAY LONG.
>
> How can I be praying for you guys today?

HOW ABOUT YOU?

> Today, I Am...

JULY 30

I AM CONFIDENCE IN HIM

TONY

> "In any and every circumstance, I have learned the secret ... I can do all things through Him who strengthens me" (Philippians 4:12-13).
>
> All leaves nothing out, no exceptions.
>
> I Am confidence in Him all day.
>
> Bless you both! Thank you for blessing me daily.

CURTIS

> Confidence in Him—you ARE, Tony! Love it! You boys inspire me every day. Thank you. I am so blessed to be friends with you.

HOW ABOUT YOU?

> Today, I Am...

JULY 31

I AM FREE, WITH GOD AS GOD IS WITH US

ETHAN

> In John 8:36, Jesus said, "if the Son sets you free, you are truly free."
>
> My heart sings today, I Am free. The world and everything in it has no grip on me. All day long!

CURTIS

> Ethan, you are free!
>
> How perfect is today's reading ...?
>
> "I also tell you this: if two of you agree here on earth concerning anything you ask, my Father in heaven will do it for you. For where two or three gather together as my followers, I am there among them" (Matthew 18:19-20).
>
> Today I Am with God as God is always with us, as we agree and ask together each day.

ETHAN

> Love it, Curtis. What a great promise tied to fellowship with other believers!

HOW ABOUT YOU?

> Today, I Am...

AUGUST 1

I AM INSTRUCTED, TRUST (IN HIM ALONE)

CURTIS

"I will instruct you and teach you in the way you should go; I will counsel you and watch over you" (Psalms 32:8).

Today I Am instructed in the way I should go! I love the definiteness of this because I need it.

ETHAN

Good morning, mighty men. A simple Proverb: "Trusting in the Lord leads to prosperity" (Proverb 28:25).

I put all my trust in the Lord. He is worthy of it all. Nothing is safer or better than the steady love of God. I Am trust (in Him alone).

CURTIS

Amen, Ethan!

HOW ABOUT YOU?

Today, I Am...

AUGUST 2

I AM LAVISHED WITH HIS GRACE, WISDOM, AND UNDERSTANDING

CURTIS

"In him we have redemption through his blood, the forgiveness of sins, in accordance with the riches of God's grace that he lavished on us with all wisdom and understanding" (Ephesians 1:7-8).

Today I Am lavished with His grace, wisdom, and understanding, all day long.

TONY

Curtis, you ARE grace and wisdom and understanding, brother. Powerful!

HOW ABOUT YOU?

Today, I Am...

AUGUST 3

I AM OPEN

TONY

Happy Thursday, men. Staying in Psalms 119, I came to verse 8 today: "Open my eyes to see the wonderful truths in your instructions."

I love the word 'open.' The truth doesn't change, but I miss it if I'm not open to it.

So today I Am open. My eyes are open to see, my ears are open to hear, and my heart is open to receive His wonderful truths today.

HOW ABOUT YOU?

Today, I Am...

AUGUST 4

I AM AWAKE

ETHAN

> "I know all the things you do, and you have a reputation for being alive—but you are dead. Wake up!" (Revelation 3:1-4).
>
> Today, I Am awake. I love God, and I will not live in the slumber and stupor of the natural world. My spirit is awake and alive and in love with my Father. All day long!

CURTIS

> Ethan, you ARE awake, brother. All day, moment by moment, others are blessed by your awakeness.

HOW ABOUT YOU?

Today, I Am...

AUGUST 5

I AM RESTING IN HIS PRESENCE
CURTIS

> "The Lord replied, 'My Presence will go with you, and I will give you rest'" (Exodus 33:14).
>
> Today I Am resting in His presence all day long.

HOW ABOUT YOU?

Today, I Am...

AUGUST 6

I AM MUSTARD SEED FAITH

TONY

"If you have faith as small as a mustard seed, you can say to this mulberry tree, 'Be uprooted and planted in the sea,' and it will obey you" (Luke 17:6).

I Am mustard seed faith today, and you guys are being prayed for with this faith today. Bless you both!

HOW ABOUT YOU?

Today, I Am...

AUGUST 7

I AM NEAR THE LORD

ETHAN

> In Deuteronomy 4:6-7, Moses says farewell to the people, knowing that, although he can see the promised land, he may not enter it. He says, "Obey (God's decrees) completely, and you will display your wisdom and intelligence among the surrounding nations ... For what great nation has a God as near to them as the Lord our God is near to us whenever we call on Him?"
>
> I Am near the Lord. He sees my every step. And He loves me.

HOW ABOUT YOU?

Today, I Am...

AUGUST 8

I AM PLEASING TO HIM

TONY

> 1 Tim 2:2-3 encourages us to pray so that "we may lead a peaceful and quiet life, godly and dignified in every way. This is good, and it is pleasing in the sight of God."
>
> I Am pleasing to Him, all day.
>
> Love you both.

CURTIS

> Tony, that was a beautiful Scripture, and you personify that truth with your life. I see it. You ARE pleasing to Him.

HOW ABOUT YOU?

> Today, I Am...

AUGUST 9

I AM WATCHED OVER

CURTIS

"I am with you and will watch over you wherever you go, and I will bring you back to this land. I will not leave you until I have done what I have promised you" (Genesis 28:15).

Today I Am watched over while God is doing what He promised. Amen!

TONY

Very powerful, Curtis. You ARE watched over and He keeps ALL of His promises. How comforting is that?!

HOW ABOUT YOU?

Today, I Am...

AUGUST 10

I AM EVER-BLESSED

ETHAN

> Love this truth from God's word and I claim it for us today: "If you fully obey the Lord ... wherever you go and whatever you do, you will be blessed" (Deuteronomy 28:1-6).
>
> Today, I Am ever-blessed. My obedience blesses God who blesses me in everything. Unspeakable joy. Hallelujah. Love you guys!

HOW ABOUT YOU?

Today, I Am...

AUGUST 11

I AM STRONG AND COURAGEOUS

CURTIS

> "Be strong and courageous. Do not be afraid or terrified because of them, for the Lord your God goes with you; he will never leave you nor forsake you" (Deuteronomy 31:6).
>
> Today I Am strong and courageous, all day long!

HOW ABOUT YOU?

Today, I Am...

AUGUST 12

I AM TRUST IN HIM

TONY

Psalms 4, short and sweet and powerful, exhorts us: "The Lord hears when I call to Him ... put your trust in the Lord."

Jesus often would pray before a miracle was performed, "Father, I thank you that you have heard me" (John 11:41).

Today He hears us; I Am trust in Him all day.

HOW ABOUT YOU?

Today, I Am...

AUGUST 13

I AM WALKING IN THE LIGHT OF HIS PRESENCE

CURTIS

"Blessed are those who have learned to acclaim you,
who walk in the light of your presence, O Lord.
They rejoice in your name all day long;
they exult in your righteousness" (Psalms 89:15-16).

Today I Am walking in the light of His presence all day long.

HOW ABOUT YOU?

Today, I Am...

AUGUST 14

I AM BLESSED

TONY

I love Ephesians 2:4-5: "But God, being rich in mercy, because of the great love with which he loved us, even when we were dead in our trespasses, made us alive together with Christ."

He is rich in mercy and has great love for us. We are alive with Christ. I Am blessed all day.

HOW ABOUT YOU?

Today, I Am...

AUGUST 15

I AM FAITH

ETHAN

On the Sabbath, Jesus went into the Synagogue and began to teach. "The people were amazed at his teaching, for he taught with real authority—quite unlike the teachers of religious law" (Mark 1:22).

The difference wasn't the material; both taught from the Old Testament. But only Jesus knew the power and truth of what He spoke on. His faith and confidence made the words come alive and be real and powerful to the listeners—to the point of amazement. Our words will only have as much power as we have faith in them.

Today, I Am faith. All my words will be activated by my faith and have real power to love and save today.

TONY

Ethan, you ARE faith all day. And may your thoughts, words, and actions be in sync with the faith and power that you ARE. Love it!

HOW ABOUT YOU?

Today, I Am...

AUGUST 16

I AM FULL OF HIS INCOMPARABLY GREAT POWER

CURTIS

> "I pray also that the eyes of your heart may be enlightened in order that you may know the hope to which He has called you, the riches of His glorious inheritance in the saints, and His incomparably great power for us who believe. That power is like the working of His mighty strength, which he exerted in Christ when He raised him from the dead and seated him at his right hand in the heavenly realms" (Ephesians 1:18-20).
>
> Today I Am full of His incomparably great power all day long.

HOW ABOUT YOU?

Today, I Am...

AUGUST 17

I AM GRATEFUL AND WORSHIP

TONY

> Hebrews 12:28 proclaims, "Let us be grateful for receiving a kingdom that cannot be shaken, and thus let us offer to God acceptable worship, with reverence and awe."
>
> I Am grateful and worship today. Double shot Tuesday.

CURTIS

> Tony, you absolutely ARE grateful and worship every day.

HOW ABOUT YOU?

> Today, I Am...

AUGUST 18

I AM LOVE

ETHAN

"God is Love" (1 John 4:8).

Today, I am joining God, declaring that I Am love. The world needs it. People have no idea how loved they are. I'm bringing it today!

Love you, brothers!

HOW ABOUT YOU?

Today, I Am...

AUGUST 19

I AM LISTENING TO GOD

ETHAN

Jesus said, "To those who listen to my teaching, more understanding will be given. But for those who are not listening, even what little understanding will be taken away from them" (Mark 4:25).

Understanding isn't something we can self-produce. He gives it, and He can take it away. Our role is simple, to listen.

Today, I Am listening to God, and thankful that He speaks to me.

HOW ABOUT YOU?

Today, I Am...

AUGUST 20

I AM GRACIOUSLY GIVEN ALL THINGS

CURTIS

"He who did not spare his own Son, but gave him up for us all—how will he not also, along with him, graciously give us all things?" (Romans 8:32).

Today I Am graciously given all things, from my Father who knows exactly what I need.

HOW ABOUT YOU?

Today, I Am...

AUGUST 21

I AM ABUNDANCE

TONY

Morning! "You have brought us out to a place of abundance" (Psalms 66:12).

No accident I came across this word today for us! Simply today, I Am abundance, all day long!

HOW ABOUT YOU?

Today, I Am...

AUGUST 22

I AM CAPABLE OF ANYTHING

ETHAN

> It's a very happy day because of Him. At the burning bush, in Exodus 3:11-12, Moses asked God, "Who am I?" And God replied, "I will certainly be with you."
>
> Anyone plus God is enough for anything. Just ask Gideon, or even Lazarus.
>
> I Am capable of anything.

HOW ABOUT YOU?

> Today, I Am...

AUGUST 23

I AM COMMITTED TO STUDYING, LIVING, AND TEACHING

CURTIS

"Ezra had committed himself to studying the Revelation of God, to living it, and to teaching Israel to live its truths and ways" (Ezra 7:8-10).

Today I Am committed to studying, living and teaching the revelation of God.

HOW ABOUT YOU?

Today, I Am...

AUGUST 24

I AM JOY AND STRENGTH

TONY

> Reading Nehemiah today and love this nugget: "For the joy of the Lord is your strength" (Nehemiah 8:10).
>
> I Am joy and strength today.

ETHAN

> Tony, you ARE joyful and strong. That's how He made you, and it's who you ARE!

HOW ABOUT YOU?

Today, I Am...

AUGUST 25

I AM PRAISE

TONY

> Philippians 4:8 is beautiful and full of awesomeness. Today I cherish this: "Whatever is pure, whatever is honorable, whatever is just, whatever is lovely, whatever is commendable, if there is any excellence, if there is anything worthy of praise, think about these things."
>
> He is ALL of these, and today I Am praise. I magnify Him, nothing else ... all day.
>
> Love you both!

HOW ABOUT YOU?

Today, I Am...

AUGUST 26

I AM FEARLESS AND FAITHFUL

ETHAN

When Jesus woke up in Mark 4:39, he rebuked the wind. Then He asked his disciples in 4:40, "Why are you afraid? Do you still have no faith?"

Fear and faith cannot occupy the same place, like light and darkness; you either have one or the other.

Today I Am fearLESS and faithFUL.

I love you both whole-heartedly and pray over all your affairs.

HOW ABOUT YOU?

Today, I Am...

AUGUST 27

I AM DELIGHTING IN HONORING OUR GOD

CURTIS

>"'O Master, listen to me, listen to your servant's prayer—and yes, to all your servants who delight in honoring you—and make me successful today so that I get what I want from the king.' I was cupbearer to the king" (Nehemiah 1:10-11).
>
>Today I Am delighting in honoring our God, all day long!

HOW ABOUT YOU?

Today, I Am...

AUGUST 28

I AM DOING A GREAT WORK

CURTIS

> Nehemiah provides our example when we are about God's business: "I'm doing a great work; I can't come down. Why should the work come to a standstill just so I can come down to see you?" (Nehemiah 6:2-3).
>
> Today I Am doing a great work and not getting distracted by the things of this world.

HOW ABOUT YOU?

> Today, I Am...

AUGUST 29

I AM STILL

ETHAN

Psalms 46:10 is short but powerful: "Be still and know that I AM God."

It provides our identity statement and His. I Am still. He IS God. And the more I comprehend His identity—GOD—the easier it is to understand mine. I Am still, all day long.

HOW ABOUT YOU?

Today, I Am...

AUGUST 30

I AM NEW IN HIM

TONY

Part of my daily reading today was Revelations 21. I love it, and I love this promise, verse 5: "Behold I am making all things new."

I Am new in Him and I want to share that with all with whom I come into contact today.

CURTIS

Love it, Tony. You ARE new. Free. Unlimited. That's YOU.

HOW ABOUT YOU?

Today, I Am...

AUGUST 31

I AM ENCOURAGED IN HEART AND UNITED IN LOVE

CURTIS

"My purpose is that they may be encouraged in heart and united in love, so that they may have the full riches of complete understanding, in order that they may know the mystery of God, namely, Christ, in whom are hidden all the treasures of wisdom and knowledge" (Colossians 2:2-3).

Today I Am encouraged in heart and united in love, all day long.

HOW ABOUT YOU?

Today, I Am...

SEPTEMBER 1

I AM LIGHT

ETHAN

> "Would anyone light a lamp and then put it under a basket? ... Of course not! A lamp is placed on a stand, where its light will shine" (Mark 4:21).
>
> As a citizen of the Kingdom, I am responsible for putting the light on a stand. Today, I Am light, shining for God.

HOW ABOUT YOU?

> Today, I Am...

SEPTEMBER 2

I AM IMITATING HIM AND WALKING IN LOVE

TONY

"Therefore be imitators of God ... and walk in love" (Ephesians 5:1-2).

It is a double shot day for me. I Am imitating Him and walking in love all day.

HOW ABOUT YOU?

Today, I Am...

SEPTEMBER 3

I AM STRENGTHENED AND UPHELD

CURTIS

"So do not fear, for I am with you;
do not be dismayed, for I am your God.
I will strengthen you and help you;
I will uphold you with my righteous right hand" (Isaiah 41:10).

Today I Am strengthened and upheld by His righteous right hand.

HOW ABOUT YOU?

Today, I Am...

SEPTEMBER 4

I AM FASCINATED BY GOD

ETHAN

In Judges 13:17-18, an angel of the Lord visits Manoah, Samson's father, and speaks prophecy over his son. Manoah then asks, "What is your name?" And God says, "It is too wonderful for you to understand."

Love this! The Lord is the creator of all that has a name, but He is simply I AM. And it IS too wonderful to understand. Thank you, God.

Today, I Am fascinated by God (and God alone).

HOW ABOUT YOU?

Today, I Am...

SEPTEMBER 5

I AM BOLD FAITH

TONY

God says to Abraham, "Fear not, Abram, I am your shield; your reward shall be very great ... and he believed the Lord, and he counted it to him as righteousness" (Genesis 15:1-6).

God wants us to trust Him and have faith in Him; that is righteousness in His eyes.

I am fearless today, because I Am bold faith all day.

HOW ABOUT YOU?

Today, I Am...

SEPTEMBER 6

I AM FREELY LOVING

ETHAN

> Jesus said, "The Sabbath was made to meet the needs of people, and not the people to meet the requirements of the Sabbath" (Mark 2:27).
>
> God loves us. He is for us. Even His rules are for us. We are way more important to Him than His rules. He loves us even if we break them. And if we're breaking a rule to love someone (like healing on the Sabbath), God wants us to. He is not a lover of rules; He is a lover of people.
>
> Today, I Am freely loving, and no rules line up against that!

HOW ABOUT YOU?

Today, I Am...

SEPTEMBER 7

I AM LISTENING

CURTIS

"The Sovereign Lord has given me an instructed tongue, to know the word that sustains the weary. He wakens me morning by morning, wakens my ear to listen like one being taught" (Isaiah 50:4).

Today I Am listening because I want to learn everything He is teaching!

HOW ABOUT YOU?

Today, I Am...

SEPTEMBER 8

I AM THANKFUL

TONY

So much awesomeness in the entire book of James 1, but here is a nugget for our day, from verse 17: "Every good gift and every perfect gift is from above, coming down from the Father."

I Am thankful again today, all day long. Abundant gifts for each of us today. Amen!

HOW ABOUT YOU?

Today, I Am...

SEPTEMBER 9

I AM CELEBRATING THE LORD'S PRESENCE

ETHAN

"David and all the people of Israel were celebrating before the Lord, singing songs and playing all kinds of musical instruments" (2 Samuel 6:5). Today, I Am celebrating the Lord's presence. With song, service and smile!

CURTIS

We are celebrating with you, Ethan!

TONY

I love it! You ARE celebration, brother, moment by moment!

HOW ABOUT YOU?

Today, I Am...

SEPTEMBER 10

I AM OVERFLOWING WITH HOPE
CURTIS

"May the God of hope fill you with all joy and peace as you trust in him, so that you may overflow with hope by the power of the Holy Spirit" (Romans 15:13).

Today I Am overflowing with hope by the power of the Holy Spirit!

HOW ABOUT YOU?

Today, I Am...

SEPTEMBER 11

I AM ANXIETY FREE

TONY

> "Therefore I tell you, do not be anxious about your life" (Matthew 6:25).
>
> Wow, straight from the mouth of Jesus. Today, I Am anxiety free because I choose faith all day long.
>
> Bless you both!

HOW ABOUT YOU?

> Today, I Am...

SEPTEMBER 12

I AM OBTAINING FRESH JOY

CURTIS

"The meek shall obtain fresh joy in the Lord, and the neediest people shall exult in the Holy One of Israel" (Isaiah 29:10).

Today I Am obtaining fresh joy through my attitude of meekness, trusting God's plan and provision.

TONY

Curtis, you ARE fresh joy, and you give it out.

HOW ABOUT YOU?

Today, I Am...

SEPTEMBER 13

I AM IN THE SPIRIT

TONY

> "The Spirit of the Lord shall rest upon him, the Spirit of wisdom and understanding, the Spirit of counsel and might, the Spirit of knowledge" (Isaiah 11:2).
>
> I Am in the Spirit today. All day. May it rest upon me.
>
> Love you guys.

ETHAN

> That Spirit rests on you, Tony, like a dove on your shoulder. All day.

HOW ABOUT YOU?

> Today, I Am...

SEPTEMBER 14

I AM ALL CONTENT

ETHAN

> Paul said in Philippians 4:12, "I have learned the secret of being content in all circumstances."
>
> Today I Am all content. Life is a symphony of joy for me.

HOW ABOUT YOU?

Today, I Am...

SEPTEMBER 15

I AM PEACE

TONY

> In John 14:27, Jesus spoke and said, "Peace I leave with you; my peace I give to you ... let not your hearts be troubled, neither let them be afraid."
>
> I accept His gift of peace; I hold it close all day. I Am peace.
>
> Love you both.

HOW ABOUT YOU?

> Today, I Am...

SEPTEMBER 16

I AM CONTROLLED BY THE SPIRIT

CURTIS

"The mind of sinful man is death, but the mind controlled by the Spirit is life and peace" (Romans 8:6).

Today I Am controlled by the Spirit, full of life and peace!

HOW ABOUT YOU?

Today, I Am...

SEPTEMBER 17

I AM CELEBRATION

ETHAN

> "God created all things, and he holds all things together" (Colossians 1:17).
>
> Thank you, God! Everywhere we look, God is ruling and reigning. Today, I Am celebration, delighting in God's mastery.

HOW ABOUT YOU?

> Today, I Am...

SEPTEMBER 18

I AM OVERFLOWING

TONY

> Morning, gents! Happy day to you both. What a great week to celebrate Jesus. I'm borrowing this one short verse today from Psalms 23:5: "My cup overflows."
>
> I Am overflowing today with thanks and love. All day long.

HOW ABOUT YOU?

Today, I Am...

SEPTEMBER 19

I AM OVERSHADOWED

CURTIS

"The angel answered, 'The Holy Spirit will come upon you, and the power of the Most High will overshadow you. So the holy one to be born will be called the Son of God'" (Luke 1:35).

Today I Am overshadowed with the power of the Most High. He is more radiant than the sun and directs me all day long.

HOW ABOUT YOU?

Today, I Am…

SEPTEMBER 20

I AM SAFETY EVERLASTING

ETHAN

David told Saul, after he cut off a piece of Saul's robe, "The Lord is my advocate, and He will rescue me from your power" (1 Samuel 24:15).

David put all his confidence in the Lord. And so do I.

I Am safety everlasting. I receive it from the Lord, I Am it, and I give it out to this world.

CURTIS

Awesome Ethan, love it! You ARE and you DO, moment by moment, all day.

HOW ABOUT YOU?

Today, I Am...

SEPTEMBER 21

I AM TRUST

TONY

> Isaiah 40 is an awesome chapter, and so much to hold onto. For me today, I choose this nugget, verse 28: "His understanding is unsearchable."
>
> He knows all, understands all, and His knowing isn't searchable to us. That means I choose to trust Him, for he knows all.
>
> Today I Am trust, and per Proverbs 3, I will acknowledge Him in all my ways.
>
> Bless you both.

HOW ABOUT YOU?

> Today, I Am...

SEPTEMBER 22

I AM BOWING DOWN IN WORSHIP

CURTIS

"Come, let us bow down in worship,
let us kneel before the Lord our Maker;
for he is our God and we are the people of his pasture,
the flock under his care" (Psalms 95:6-7).

Today I Am bowing down in worship, grateful for His almighty care!

HOW ABOUT YOU?

Today, I Am...

SEPTEMBER 23

I AM LISTENING TO YOU

ETHAN

"Then you will call on me and come and pray to me, and I will listen to you" (Jeremiah 29:12).

Father, today I Am listening to You! Make me Your instrument for Your glory.

HOW ABOUT YOU?

Today, I Am...

SEPTEMBER 24

I AM WALKING BY FAITH

CURTIS

"For we walk by faith, not by sight" (2 Corinthians 5:7).

Today I Am walking by faith all day long!

HOW ABOUT YOU?

Today, I Am...

SEPTEMBER 25

I AM STEADFAST, TRUSTING IN THE LORD

ETHAN

Today, I share a verse I clung to for comfort the summer I studied for the bar exam, Psalms 112:7: "He has no fear of bad news whose heart is steadfast trusting in the Lord."

That was me then, and that is me today.

I Am steadfast, trusting in the Lord. As such, everything is different; light is everywhere; and I rejoice at seeing abundance in all directions. Love you guys so much!

CURTIS

Love it, Ethan! Steadfast you ARE!

HOW ABOUT YOU?

Today, I Am...

SEPTEMBER 26

I AM TRUST IN HIM

TONY

Looking at Psalms 25:1, I love these four words: "In you I trust."

Enough said. Today I Am trust in Him, all-in trust, moment-by-moment this day.

Bless you both!

HOW ABOUT YOU?

Today, I Am...

SEPTEMBER 27

I AM IN PERFECT PEACE

CURTIS

"You will keep in perfect peace him whose mind is steadfast, because he trusts in you. Trust in the Lord forever, for the Lord, the Lord, is the Rock eternal" (Isaiah 26:3-4).

Today I Am in perfect peace because I trust in our Lord forever! Way to lead us, Isaiah.

HOW ABOUT YOU?

Today, I Am...

SEPTEMBER 28

I AM MIRACLE-FAITH

ETHAN

> Mark 6:5 talks about Jesus in His hometown: "And because of their unbelief, he couldn't do any miracles among them." Contrast this with the previous chapter where a lady, by faith, pulled healing from Jesus' robe (Mark 5:27).
>
> Today, I Am miracle-faith. I know miracles happen and it's through our faith that God creates them. Blessings to you both today!

HOW ABOUT YOU?

Today, I Am...

SEPTEMBER 29

I AM STANDING FIRM IN HIM

TONY

> Philippians 4:1 is my verse for today; I love this whole chapter, but today I choose the opening: "Stand firm thus in the Lord."
>
> I Am standing firm in Him all day.

HOW ABOUT YOU?

> Today, I Am...

SEPTEMBER 30

I AM OVERFLOWING WITH HOPE AND ABUNDANT LOVE

CURTIS

"May the God of hope fill you with all joy and peace as you trust in him, so that you may overflow with hope by the power of the Holy Spirit" (Romans 15:13).

Today I Am overflowing with hope and abundant love, all day long!

HOW ABOUT YOU?

Today, I Am...

OCTOBER 1

I AM RADIANT

ETHAN

Good morning, men. I'm praying for your days.

"His face had become radiant because he had spoken with the Lord" (Exodus 34:29).

Today, I Am radiant because I have spoken with the Lord this morning. Love you guys.

CURTIS

Ethan, you are radiant; in fact your whole family is!

HOW ABOUT YOU?

Today, I Am...

OCTOBER 2

I AM DEVOTED TO PRAYER

CURTIS

"Devote yourselves to prayer, being watchful and thankful" (Colossians 4:2).

Today I Am devoted to prayer, all day long.

TONY

You ARE devoted to prayer, Curtis. Your life-song sings of it every day.

HOW ABOUT YOU?

Today, I Am...

OCTOBER 3

I AM DELIVERED

TONY

Psalms 54:7 declares, "For He has delivered me from every trouble."

This is an amazing and wonderful truth; I give thanks, and today, I Am delivered. Bless you both.

HOW ABOUT YOU?

Today, I Am...

OCTOBER 4

I AM UNLIMITED

ETHAN

> "Now to Him who is able to do far more abundantly than all that we ask or think, according to the power at work within us" (Ephesians 3:20).
>
> No limits. None! I Am unlimited and so ARE you.
>
> Your day, all your affairs, are being lifted up in prayer for abundant miracles, exceeding all you can ask or think.
>
> Love you both.

HOW ABOUT YOU?

Today, I Am...

OCTOBER 5

I AM REMAINING IN JESUS

CURTIS

"If you remain in me and my words remain in you, ask whatever you wish, and it will be given you" (John 15:4-7).

Today I Am remaining in Jesus, loving His presence.

HOW ABOUT YOU?

Today, I Am...

OCTOBER 6

I AM FAITHFULNESS

TONY

Here is another good word from the Psalms; it fits nicely.

"Steadfast love and faithfulness meet ... yes, the Lord will give what is good" (Psalms 85:10-12).

I Am faithfulness today. And may the Lord keep his promise to all of us today and give what is good.

Bless you both.

CURTIS

You ARE faithfulness, Tony. Thanks for reminding us of that good promise.

HOW ABOUT YOU?

Today, I Am...

OCTOBER 7

I AM GETTING WISDOM

CURTIS

"Above all and before all, do this: Get Wisdom! Write this at the top of your list: Get Understanding! Throw your arms around her—believe me, you won't regret it; never let her go—she'll make your life glorious" (Proverbs 4: 3-9).

Today I Am getting wisdom all day long!

HOW ABOUT YOU?

Today, I Am...

OCTOBER 8

I AM A LOUD VOICE FOR THE LORD

ETHAN

One of the coolest things in all the Bible: the people "shouted as loud as they could. Suddenly, the walls of Jericho collapsed, and the Israelites charged straight into the town and captured it" (Joshua 6:20).

Today, I Am a loud voice for the Lord; walls will fall and God's kingdom will expand.

HOW ABOUT YOU?

Today, I Am...

OCTOBER 9

I AM STRONG AND COURAGEOUS

TONY

> My reading today brought me to one of my favorite stories in the Bible, where Joshua is commissioned by God. Josh 1:9, my word of the day, says, "Have I not commanded you? Be strong and courageous. Do not be frightened, and do not be dismayed, for the Lord your God is with you wherever you go."
>
> I love this, every word of it. Today, I Am strong and courageous.

HOW ABOUT YOU?

> Today, I Am...

OCTOBER 10

I AM CENTERED WITH CHRIST

CURTIS

> "Before you know it, a sense of God's wholeness, everything coming together for good, will come and settle you down. It's wonderful what happens when Christ displaces worry at the center of your life" (Philippians 4:7).
>
> Today I Am centered with Christ, all day long.

HOW ABOUT YOU?

Today, I Am...

OCTOBER 11

I AM BOLD

ETHAN

Most days I find a Scripture I like and get my identity from it. But I work from the Scripture back. Today, I did the reverse and found a Scripture to fit my identity.

I felt bold, and I declared I Am bold.

ETHAN

And then Proverbs 28:1 says, "The wicked flee (even) when no one pursues them, but the righteous are as bold as a lion."

I Am bold. I stand my ground. I declare the gospel. I set my heart on love and it will not be shaken. I shine brighter today. Boldly!

HOW ABOUT YOU?

Today, I Am...

OCTOBER 12

I AM THANKS

TONY

2 Chronicles 30:9 contains a powerful truth, as spoken by Hezekiah when he became king: "The Lord your God is gracious and merciful and will not turn his face away from you."

Today, I Am thanks, all day. The list is too long to say but I will start with being thankful for His grace and mercy.

Bless you both.

HOW ABOUT YOU?

Today, I Am...

OCTOBER 13

I AM A GENTLE AND QUIET SPIRIT

CURTIS

"Instead, it should be that of your inner self, the unfading beauty of a gentle and quiet spirit, which is of great worth in God's sight" (1 Peter 3:4).

Today I Am a gentle and quiet spirit, sharing God's love all day long.

ETHAN

That's so good, Curtis ... a quiet and gentle spirit you ARE!

HOW ABOUT YOU?

Today, I Am...

OCTOBER 14

I AM FULLNESS FOREVERMORE

ETHAN

> Love this old school translation of Psalms 16:11: "in thy presence is fullness of joy; at thy right hand there are pleasures forevermore."
>
> I Am fullness forevermore because His presence is always with me. My cup runneth over.

HOW ABOUT YOU?

Today, I Am...

OCTOBER 15

I AM TRANSFORMED INTO HIS LIKENESS

CURTIS

"And we, who with unveiled faces all reflect the Lord's glory, are being transformed into His likeness with ever-increasing glory, which comes from the Lord, who is the Spirit" (2 Corinthians 3:18).

Today I Am transformed into His likeness with ever-increasing glory, all day long!

ETHAN

I love it, Curtis! Be transformed all day, brother!

HOW ABOUT YOU?

Today, I Am...

OCTOBER 16

I AM STRENGTH

ETHAN

> Morning, mighty men. Thankful for you both today. Love this: "My health may fail, and my spirit may grow weak, but God remains the strength of my heart; He is mine forever" (Psalms 73:26).
>
> So I Am strength today. God is the source. Forever.

TONY

> That is beautiful; God remains the strength of our hearts. You ARE strength, Ethan!

HOW ABOUT YOU?

Today, I Am...

OCTOBER 17

I AM WALKING IN THE LIGHT
TONY

> Morning, mighty men! Psalms 89:15-17 contains some beautiful excerpts of His word: "Blessed are the people ... who walk, O Lord, in the light of your face, who exult in your name all the day ... for you are the glory of their strength."
>
> This is who I Am today. I Am walking in the light of His face, exulting in His name! All day long, moment by moment.
>
> Bless you both! You ARE prayed for with the I am presence of God.

HOW ABOUT YOU?

Today, I Am...

OCTOBER 18

I AM STEADFAST

CURTIS

> "Even in darkness light dawns for the upright,
> for the gracious and compassionate and righteous man. . . .
> He will have no fear of bad news;
> his heart is steadfast, trusting in the Lord" (Psalms 112:4-7).
>
> Today I Am steadfast, trusting in the Lord!

TONY

> I love it! You ARE steadfast, trusting in Him. I see it every day from you.

HOW ABOUT YOU?

Today, I Am...

OCTOBER 19

I AM AGAIN AND AGAIN

ETHAN

"Again and again the Lord sent his prophets and seers to warn both Israel and Judah." (2 Kings 17:13).

God has an "again and again" nature! God's love is unrelenting. Today, I Am again and again. I Am an again and again husband. I Am an again and again friend. I Am again and again love to this world!

HOW ABOUT YOU?

Today, I Am...

OCTOBER 20

I AM JOY INEXPRESSIBLE

TONY

"Though you have not seen him, you love him. Though you do not now see him, you believe in him and rejoice with joy that is inexpressible" (1 Peter 1:8).

Today, I Am joy inexpressible. And you guys are PRAYED FOR!

HOW ABOUT YOU?

Today, I Am...

OCTOBER 21

I AM ACKNOWLEDGING OUR FATHER

CURTIS

> "Trust in the Lord with all your heart
> and lean not on your own understanding;
> in all your ways acknowledge him,
> and he will make your paths straight"
> (Proverbs 3:5-6).
>
> Today I Am acknowledging our Father in all my ways. I love His straight path!

TONY

> Love, love, love Proverbs 3! And you ARE acknowledging Him, all ways, always.

HOW ABOUT YOU?

Today, I Am...

OCTOBER 22

I AM STRONG

ETHAN

"The eyes of the Lord search the whole earth in order to strengthen those whose hearts are fully committed to Him" (2 Chronicles 16:9).

Today, I Am strong. I will guard my heart, set my mind on things above, and remember that Love never fails! Never means never.

HOW ABOUT YOU?

Today, I Am...

OCTOBER 23

I AM KEPT BY HIM

TONY

> I love this little nugget from Psalms 121:5: "The Lord is your keeper."
>
> I find great comfort in this truth. I Am kept by Him and by His love.

CURTIS

> Love it, Tony. You ARE kept by Him. It's true.

HOW ABOUT YOU?

> Today, I Am...

OCTOBER 24

I AM COMPLETELY KNOWN
CURTIS

"O Lord, you have searched me
and you know me.
You know when I sit and when I rise;
you perceive my thoughts from afar.
You discern my going out and my lying down;
you are familiar with all my ways.
Before a word is on my tongue
you know it completely, O Lord" (Psalms 139:1-4).

Today I Am completely known and I give my everything to Him for correction and blessing.

TONY

Curtis, you ARE completely known and are giving everything to Him; may you both be blessed every day!

HOW ABOUT YOU?

Today, I Am...

OCTOBER 25

I AM JOY

ETHAN

> Habakkuk 3 talks about how, even when adversity is all around, "Yet I will be joyful in the God of my salvation" (Habakkuk 3:18).
>
> Today, I ignore material things, abiding in the joy of the Lord. I Am joy, all day, moment by moment.

HOW ABOUT YOU?

> Today, I Am...

OCTOBER 26

I AM BLESSING HIM, LOVE
TONY

Psalms 103! The entire chapter is full of awesomeness. Verse 1 stands out: "Bless the Lord, O my soul, and all that is within me, bless his holy name."

I Am blessing Him, all day, and I am love

HOW ABOUT YOU?

Today, I Am...

OCTOBER 27

I AM SECURE

TONY

> "Whoever listens to me will dwell secure and will be at ease" (Proverbs 1:33).
>
> I Am secure, being at ease. That is me, all day.
>
> Love you both!

HOW ABOUT YOU?

> Today, I Am...

OCTOBER 28

I AM STAYED ON JESUS

CURTIS

"You will guard him and keep him in perfect and constant peace whose mind [both its inclination and its character] is stayed on You, because he commits himself to You, leans on You, and hopes confidently in You" (Isaiah 26:3).

I Am stayed on Jesus, who's keeping us in perfect and constant peace!

ETHAN

Awesome! Stayed is really good. And you ARE, all day.

HOW ABOUT YOU?

Today, I Am...

OCTOBER 29

I AM FILLED TO THE BRIM

ETHAN

> In 2 Kings 4:3-7, Elisha said to the widow, "Borrow as many empty jars as you can ... then go into your house ... shut the door behind you ... pour olive oil from your flask into the jars."
>
> "Soon every jar was full to the brim!"
>
> Elisha then said, "Now sell the olive oil and pay your debts, and you and your sons can live on what is left."
>
> Today, I recognize the abundance of God and His goodness towards me. I Am filled to the brim. What is done behind closed doors (in the secret place) is seen by all the world!

HOW ABOUT YOU?

> Today, I Am...

OCTOBER 30

I AM UNTOPPLEABLE AND UNSTOPPABLE

CURTIS

> "But the Master, God, has something to say to this: 'Watch closely. I'm laying a foundation in Zion, a solid granite foundation, squared and true. And this is the meaning of the stone: A TRUSTING LIFE WON'T TOPPLE'" (Isaiah 28:16-17).
>
> Today I Am untoppleable and unstoppable through trust in Him!

HOW ABOUT YOU?

Today, I Am...

OCTOBER 31

I AM FAITH

ETHAN

> In Samuel's farewell address to Israel, He warns them to obey the Lord's commands, and then He says this: "Now stand here and see the great thing the Lord is about to do" (1 Samuel 12:16).
>
> Today, I Am faith, standing and seeing the Lord's great works.

TONY

> You ARE faith, Ethan. It exudes from you, brother. It rubs off on me and blesses me.

HOW ABOUT YOU?

> Today, I Am...

NOVEMBER 1

I AM SAFE

TONY

> "The name of the Lord is a strong tower; the righteous man runs into it and is safe" (Proverbs 18:10).
>
> I Am safe today. No fear. All is well. You guys are prayed over—praying for abundance!

ETHAN

> Love it, Tony. You ARE safe. Peace on all sides.

HOW ABOUT YOU?

Today, I Am...

NOVEMBER 2

I AM SHAPED TO SERVE JESUS

CURTIS

"Remember these things, O Jacob. Take it seriously, Israel, that you're my servant. I made you, shaped you: You're my servant. O Israel, I'll never forget you. I've wiped the slate of all your wrongdoings. There's nothing left of your sins. Come back to me, come back. I've redeemed you" (Isaiah 44:21-22).

Today (and from the beginning of time) I Am shaped to serve Jesus. He's wiped our sins clean, and we are redeemed for His perfect plan.

ETHAN

Powerful, Curtis! You ARE shaped by and for Jesus!

TONY

Love that, Curtis! That is the truth and who you ARE!

HOW ABOUT YOU?

Today, I Am...

NOVEMBER 3

I AM HIS VICTORY

ETHAN

In 2 Samuel 7:8-9, the Lord says to David, "I took you from tending sheep in the pastures and selected you to be the leader of my people Israel. I have been wherever you have gone, and I have destroyed all your enemies before your eyes."

I claim this same type of relationship with the Lord for myself and for you today. We speak to Him, and He speaks to us. Wherever we go, He goes. He gives us victory.

Today, I Am His victory.

HOW ABOUT YOU?

Today, I Am...

NOVEMBER 4

I AM PLEASING TO HIM

TONY

> Good morning, men! Hebrews 11:6 says, "And without faith it is impossible to please Him."
>
> A beautiful nugget for today. God is pleased when we have faith in Him. How simple and cool is that?
>
> I Am pleasing to Him today with my bold faith.

HOW ABOUT YOU?

> Today, I Am...

NOVEMBER 5

I AM SHARING HIS WORD AND ACHIEVING HIS PURPOSE

CURTIS

"So is my word that goes out from my mouth: It will not return to me empty, but will accomplish what I desire and achieve the purpose for which I sent it" (Isaiah 55:11).

Today I Am sharing His word and achieving His purpose, all day long!

ETHAN

Love it, Curtis! You ARE that, in both being and doing.

HOW ABOUT YOU?

Today, I Am...

NOVEMBER 6

I AM OBEDIENCE TO HIS VOICE

TONY

Deuteronomy 28 is full of blessings for obedience, and verse 2 is so awesome: "And all these blessings shall come upon you and overtake you, if you obey the voice of the Lord your God."

I Am obedience to His voice.

HOW ABOUT YOU?

Today, I Am...

NOVEMBER 7

I AM LEARNING FROM JESUS
CURTIS

"Come to me, all you who are weary and burdened, and I will give you rest. Take my yoke upon you and learn from me, for I am gentle and humble in heart, and you will find rest for your souls" (Matthew 11:28-29).

Today I Am learning from Jesus all day long!

HOW ABOUT YOU?

Today, I Am...

NOVEMBER 8

I AM ALL IN

ETHAN

> Elijah told the widow, "There will always be flour and olive oil left in your containers" (1 Kings 17:14).
>
> She believed it on faith and gave what would have been the last of her resources. She went "all in"—and her supply continued supernaturally. Today, I Am all in. And I know (in faith) that God will multiply!

HOW ABOUT YOU?

> Today, I Am...

NOVEMBER 9

I AM ABUNDANT LIFE

TONY

"I came that they may have life and have it abundantly. I am the good shepherd" (John 10:10-11).

He IS the good shepherd, and I Am abundant life. All day!

Bless you both.

HOW ABOUT YOU?

Today, I Am...

NOVEMBER 10

I AM VISION

ETHAN

> "Elisha prayed, 'O Lord, open his eyes and let him see!' ... and when the young man looked up, he saw that the hillside around Elisha was filled with horses and chariots of fire" (2 Kings 6:17).
>
> I love this. And you and I enjoy the same heavenly protection ... we just need to see it.
>
> Today, I Am vision. Like Elisha, I see into the spirit realm, and it overrules what I perceive in the natural.

HOW ABOUT YOU?

Today, I Am...

NOVEMBER 11

I AM LIGHT

TONY

> Morning men! What a joyful day it is. And I am thankful for this day and the gift of being able to create. Love it!
>
> "May God be gracious to us and bless us and make his face to shine upon us" (Psalms 67:1).
>
> He IS grace to me, HE blesses me, HE shines upon me ... and I Am light today.
>
> Everywhere I go.

ETHAN

> Love it, Tony. You ARE light. You shine!

HOW ABOUT YOU?

> Today, I Am...

NOVEMBER 12

I AM DELIGHTING MYSELF IN THE LORD

CURTIS

"Delight yourself in the Lord
and he will give you the desires of your heart" (Psalms 37:4).

Today I Am delighting myself in the Lord; this is the desire of my heart all day long.

HOW ABOUT YOU?

Today, I Am...

NOVEMBER 13

I AM STILL

CURTIS

"Be still before the Lord, all mankind, because he has roused himself from his holy dwelling" (Zechariah 2:13).

Today I Am still before our Lord, Trusting in His plan and listening for His voice of direction.

HOW ABOUT YOU?

Today, I Am...

NOVEMBER 14

I AM RISING LIKE THE SUN

ETHAN

> Today contains millions of miracles we get to participate in. I share this verse that caught my eye this morning: "But may those who love you rise like the sun in all its power!" (Judges 5:31).
>
> I claim it—I Am rising like the sun in all its power. Love you.

TONY

> Bring it my brother. You are rising like the Son!

HOW ABOUT YOU?

> Today, I Am...

NOVEMBER 15

I AM TRUST IN HIM

TONY

> Proverbs 3 is one of my favorite chapters, and today I am this sentence in verse 5: "Trust in the Lord with all your heart."
>
> Straightforward command: I Am trust in Him today with ALL of me.

HOW ABOUT YOU?

> Today, I Am...

NOVEMBER 16

I AM EMBRACING THE NEW

CURTIS

"Therefore, if anyone is in Christ, he is a new creation; the old has gone, the new has come!" (2 Corinthians 5:17).

Today I Am embracing the New: all that God is doing in me, a new creation for His purposes.

HOW ABOUT YOU?

Today, I Am...

NOVEMBER 17

I AM RENEWED

ETHAN

> Today, I'm reminded by Romans 12:2 that transformation happens "by the renewing of your mind."
>
> Today I Am renewed—mind, body, soul, spirit. All are new. I approach this day with nothing but love and abundance, as though I were born today, discovering everything for the first time. Love you both.

HOW ABOUT YOU?

> Today, I Am...

NOVEMBER 18

I AM STRONG AND COURAGEOUS

TONY

> My word of the day is Joshua 1:9, a favorite: "Be strong and courageous. Do not be frightened, and do not be dismayed, for the Lord your God is with you wherever you go."
>
> He is my God and is with me always. I Am strong and courageous today. Look out!

HOW ABOUT YOU?

Today, I Am...

NOVEMBER 19

I AM PRAYING CONTINUALLY
CURTIS

"Pray continually" (1 Thessalonians 5:17).

Today I Am praying continually, trusting in His leading and providence.

HOW ABOUT YOU?

Today, I Am...

NOVEMBER 20

I AM HIS AMBASSADOR

TONY

I join in today from Ephesians 1:4: "Even as he chose us in him before the foundation of the world, that we should be holy and blameless before him."

He chose us before He created the earth. Wow! Today I Am His ambassador, everywhere I go, moment by moment.

You men inspire me! Thank you for your words of faith and power you continually pour into me. Love you.

HOW ABOUT YOU?

Today, I Am...

NOVEMBER 21

I AM TRUTH

ETHAN

> In John 8:32, Jesus says, "The truth shall set you free."
>
> So I'm only as free as I am truthful. Lies bind my mind, my life, my relationships—all of it.
>
> Today, I Am truth. I ask God to reveal anything that is untrue which I have accepted as truth. I am freer and freer, moment-by-moment.

HOW ABOUT YOU?

> Today, I Am...

NOVEMBER 22

I AM GIVING THANKS

CURTIS

"In everything give thanks; for this is the will of God in Christ Jesus for you" (1 Thessalonians 5:18).

Today I Am giving thanks in everything. We are so blessed, and I want to appreciate His provision more fully.

HOW ABOUT YOU?

Today, I Am...

NOVEMBER 23

I AM INTIMATE WITH GOD

ETHAN

> You've heard it said, "In all your ways acknowledge Him and He will make straight your paths" (Proverbs 3:6).
>
> But I love this translation as well: "Become intimate with Him in whatever you do, and he will lead you wherever you go."
>
> Today, I Am intimate with God.

TONY

> Bring it, brother! He loves us so!

HOW ABOUT YOU?

> Today, I Am...

NOVEMBER 24

I AM FOLLOWING JESUS

CURTIS

> "Jesus answered, 'If I want him to remain alive until I return, what is that to you? You must follow me'" (John 21:22).
>
> I'm keeping it simple. Today I Am following Jesus, all day long!

ETHAN

> I like it, Curtis! You ARE following Him. You do every day!

TONY

> Love it. You ARE following Him, Curtis!

HOW ABOUT YOU?

> Today, I Am...

NOVEMBER 25

I AM PEACE

ETHAN

Today I Am peace.

"And the peace that transcends all understanding will guard your heart and your mind in Christ Jesus" (Philippians 4:7).

There is no way to comprehend the depth of peace I have and AM today. Bless you both.

CURTIS

Ethan, may you BE peace all day in all ways.

HOW ABOUT YOU?

Today, I Am...

NOVEMBER 26

I AM WITHOUT FEAR

TONY

"Take heart; it is I. Do not be afraid" (Matthew 14:27).

Before every engagement today, I take this with me. I Am without fear, all day long.

CURTIS

Tony, you are fearless!

HOW ABOUT YOU?

Today, I Am...

NOVEMBER 27

I AM WHOLLY JOYFUL

CURTIS

"Consider it wholly joyful, my brethren, whenever you are enveloped in or encounter trials of any sort or fall into various temptations. Be assured and understand that the trial and proving of your faith bring out endurance and steadfastness and patience" (James 1:2-3).

Today I Am wholly joyful all day long!

HOW ABOUT YOU?

Today, I Am...

NOVEMBER 28

I AM UNLIMITED

ETHAN

> Jesus preached, "If someone slaps you on the right cheek, offer the other cheek also. If you are sued in court and your shirt is taken from you, give your coat, too. If a soldier demands that you carry his gear for a mile, carry it two miles" (Matthew 5:38-41).
>
> These are metaphors for comfort, which man too often seeks to protect. The lie is that there is scarcity; God's provisions are enough, and they always will be.
>
> So today I Am unlimited. Moreover, I seek to give away what God has first given me.

TONY

> I love it. Unlimited is so powerful. Awesome, brother. Thanks for sharing, and may we all enjoy miracles, and the giving of those miracles, all day long.

HOW ABOUT YOU?

> Today, I Am...

NOVEMBER 29

I AM LOVE

TONY

> Love Isaiah 33:2: "O Lord, be gracious to us; we wait for you."
>
> Love this simple request and I send it forth to our Father for us today.
>
> I Am love today, to all those I come into contact with.

ETHAN

> Tony, you are love, and we are loving you back!

HOW ABOUT YOU?

> Today, I Am...

NOVEMBER 30

I AM SEEKING HIS FACE

CURTIS

"Look to the Lord and his strength; seek his face always" (1 Chronicles 16:11).

Today I Am seeking His face all day long. I want to be His reflection to everyone I encounter.

TONY

Another favorite! BE his reflection, Curtis; touch all you come into contact with. Awesome!

HOW ABOUT YOU?

Today, I Am...

DECEMBER 1

I AM MY BROTHER'S KEEPER

TONY

In Genesis 4:9, God asked Cain where his brother was and Cain replied, "I don't know. Am I my brother's keeper?"

Today I break off from this spirit of offense as I boldly proclaim I Am my brother's keeper. When he weeps, I weep; when he thrives, I thrive. We are ONE.

HOW ABOUT YOU?

Today, I Am...

DECEMBER 2

I AM UPHELD WITH THE LORD'S HAND

CURTIS

"If the Lord delights in a man's way,
He makes his steps firm;
though he stumble, he will not fall,
for the Lord upholds him with His hand" (Psalms 37:23-24).

Today I Am upheld with the Lord's hand; my steps are firm and He delights in me!

How great He is!

HOW ABOUT YOU?

Today, I Am...

DECEMBER 3

I AM ABUNDANCE

ETHAN

"The Lord is able to give you much more than this!" (2 Chronicles 25:9).

Doesn't matter what "this" is—any "this"—the Lord is able to give much more. And He wants to! Abundance is something we only see the outer fringes of. Extravagance incomprehensible.

Because of His presence, I Am abundance today.

HOW ABOUT YOU?

Today, I Am...

DECEMBER 4

I AM THANKS FOR THE GIFT OF VICTORY

TONY

> Today I am reminded of this powerful verse from 1 Corinthians 15:57, "but thanks be to God, who gives us the victory through our Lord Jesus Christ."
>
> I Am thanks today for the gift of victory.

CURTIS

> You ARE thanks, Tony. I see it. And you ARE victory. I see that too. And today is yours to seize. Go out and take it.

HOW ABOUT YOU?

> Today, I Am...

DECEMBER 5

I AM FILLED TO THE MEASURE
CURTIS

"So that Christ may dwell in your hearts through faith. And I pray that you, being rooted and established in love, may have power, together with all the saints, to grasp how wide and long and high and deep is the love of Christ, and to know this love that surpasses knowledge—that you may be filled to the measure of all the fullness of God" (Ephesians 3:17-19).

Today I Am filled to the measure of all the fullness of God!

HOW ABOUT YOU?

Today, I Am...

DECEMBER 6

I AM STILL

ETHAN

> Today, I return to this great truth from Psalms 46:10: "Be still and know that I am God."
>
> Today I Am still. I Am still. He is responsible for increase. Not me. He multiplies. Not me. I know that He IS God.
>
> So I Am still.

HOW ABOUT YOU?

> Today, I Am...

DECEMBER 7

I AM TRUST

TONY

I leave you today with Luke 12:22.

Jesus spoke, "Do not be anxious about your life."

Love it! Simple and a command I accept. I Am trust all day.

HOW ABOUT YOU?

Today, I Am...

DECEMBER 8

I AM WORSHIPPING GOD

CURTIS

> "Therefore, since we are receiving a kingdom that cannot be shaken, let us be thankful, and so worship God acceptably with reverence and awe, for our 'God is a consuming fire'" (Hebrews 12:28-29).
>
> Today I Am worshipping God with reverence and awe. He is our consuming fire!

HOW ABOUT YOU?

> Today, I Am...

DECEMBER 9

I AM ABIDING IN HIS SHADOW

TONY

Psalms 91! So much awesomeness in this chapter. I hold onto verse 1 today, it is who I Am.

"He who dwells in the shelter of the Most High will abide in the shadow of the Almighty."

I Am abiding in His shadow.

HOW ABOUT YOU?

Today, I Am...

DECEMBER 10

I AM SMILING

ETHAN

> When Jacob and Esau are reunited in Genesis 33:10, Jacob says, "What a relief to see your friendly smile. It is like seeing the face of God!"
>
> Today I Am smiling. People will see the face of God—the face of love and grace and forgiveness.

HOW ABOUT YOU?

> Today, I Am...

DECEMBER 11

I AM KEPT IN PERFECT PEACE

CURTIS

"You will keep him in perfect peace,
Whose mind is stayed on You,
Because he trusts in You" (Isaiah 26:3).

Today I Am kept in perfect peace, all day long.

HOW ABOUT YOU?

Today, I Am...

DECEMBER 12

I AM ACCEPTANCE

ETHAN

> "Job scraped his skin with a piece of broken pottery as he sat among the ashes. His wife said to him 'Are you still trying to maintain your integrity? Curse God and die.' But Job replied ' ... Should we accept only good things from the hand of God and never anything bad?'" (Job 2:8-10).
>
> Powerful words. Today, I Am acceptance.
>
> Accepting good and bad things from the hand of God demonstrates faith. Job's faith is amazing. We can't see the future, so we just have to lean on our faith that God loves us.

HOW ABOUT YOU?

Today, I Am...

DECEMBER 13

I AM FILLED WITH GOD'S EXCELLENT POWER

CURTIS

"But we have this treasure in earthen vessels, that the excellence of the power may be of God and not of us" (2 Corinthians 4:7).

Today I Am filled with God's excellent power!

ETHAN

I love it, Curtis. You ARE filled with God's excellent power! And that is awesome beyond words.

HOW ABOUT YOU?

Today, I Am...

DECEMBER 14

I AM DEEPEST AWE

ETHAN

> Psalms 5:5 says, "The proud may not stand in your presence," but 5:7 says, "I will worship at your Temple with deepest awe."
>
> I Am deepest awe. For our Lord and all His creation. Praise God that this posture allows us into His presence. There's no place I'd rather be.

HOW ABOUT YOU?

> Today, I Am...

DECEMBER 15

I AM DRAWING NEAR

TONY

"Let us then with confidence draw near to the throne of grace, that we may receive mercy and find grace to help in time of need" (Hebrews 4:16).

I love this word and want to be mindful of it all day. I Am drawing near to throne of grace all day long.

HOW ABOUT YOU?

Today, I Am...

DECEMBER 16

I AM HIS WORKMANSHIP
CURTIS

> "Yet, O Lord, you are our Father.
> We are the clay, you are the potter;
> we are all the work of your hand" (Isaiah 64:8).
>
> Today I Am His workmanship, and I simply want to submit to His hand all day long.

HOW ABOUT YOU?

Today, I Am...

DECEMBER 17

I AM WORKING FOR THE LORD

CURTIS

> Solid advice: "Whatever you do, work at it with all your heart, as working for the Lord, not for men" (Colossians 3:23).
>
> Today I Am working for the Lord!

HOW ABOUT YOU?

> Today, I Am...

DECEMBER 18

I AM AFRESH WITH THE KNOWLEDGE OF GOD

ETHAN

Good morning, men! Another miraculous day is upon us! In Exodus 6:2-3, God says to Moses, "I appeared to Abraham, Isaac and Jacob as God Almighty (El-Shaddai), but by my name Yahweh (God is Present) I was not known to them."

God is saying that, although they were the fathers of the nation, He is revealing himself as something new to Moses. God loves to reveal new things about Himself to us.

Today, I Am afresh with the knowledge of God.

HOW ABOUT YOU?

Today, I Am...

DECEMBER 19

I AM LOVED EVERLASTINGLY

CURTIS

"The Lord appeared to us in the past, saying: 'I have loved you with an everlasting love; I have drawn you with loving-kindness'" (Jeremiah 31:3).

Most importantly, today I Am loved everlastingly (and regardless of my performance) by our Heavenly Father.

ETHAN

Yes, yes, yes, Curtis! You ARE loved. Truth.

HOW ABOUT YOU?

Today, I Am...

DECEMBER 20

I AM THRIVING IN THE HOUSE OF GOD

ETHAN

> "I am like an olive tree, thriving in the house of God" (Psalms 52:8).
>
> That is me! I Am thriving in the House of God. Everywhere I go! Love you guys and appreciate your faithful friendship.

CURTIS

> Ethan is thriving, all day long!

HOW ABOUT YOU?

Today, I Am...

DECEMBER 21

I AM WORSHIPPING GOD WITH REVERENCE AND AWE

CURTIS

"Therefore, since we are receiving a kingdom that cannot be shaken, let us be thankful, and so worship God acceptably with reverence and awe, for our 'God is a consuming fire'" (Hebrews 12:28-29).

Today I Am worshipping God with reverence and awe. He deserves all the glory!

HOW ABOUT YOU?

Today, I Am...

DECEMBER 22

I AM HEARING GOD'S WHISPERS

ETHAN

"And after the fire there was the sound of a gentle whisper" (1 Kings 19:12).

Elijah heard God in that gentle whisper and did what God instructed. Today, I Am hearing God's whispers and obeying. Love you guys.

HOW ABOUT YOU?

Today, I Am...

DECEMBER 23

I AM LETTING GOD SET THE PACE

CURTIS

In Romans 3:27-28, Paul reminds us who is running the show: "What we've learned is this: God does not respond to what we do; we respond to what God does. We've finally figured it out. Our lives get in step with God and all others by letting him set the pace, not by proudly or anxiously trying to run the parade."

Today I Am letting God set the pace. I'd rather be in His parade than mine every time!

HOW ABOUT YOU?

Today, I Am...

DECEMBER 24

I AM THANKFUL, WITH GOD

TONY

> Matthew 1:23 says, "And they shall call His name Immanuel (which means, God with us)."
>
> I Am thankful for this gift, all day long. He lives in us, wow!

ETHAN

> Good morning. Thank you, Tony, for BEING thankful. See it in all you say and do. I love that Jesus is Immanuel, God with us. Today I am with God, because of Jesus, and because of your friendships, which I truly cherish.

HOW ABOUT YOU?

Today, I Am...

DECEMBER 25

I AM THANKFUL

CURTIS

> I love that God is with us. I Am thankful all day long!
>
> "Let the peace of Christ rule in your hearts, since as members of one body you were called to peace. And be thankful" (Colossians 3:15).
>
> Merry Christmas, brothers! We are loved by Christ our King!!

TONY

> Merry Christmas, brothers! Loving you!

ETHAN

> Merry Christmas to my brothers and your families. Love you!

HOW ABOUT YOU?

> Today, I Am...

DECEMBER 26

I AM CLINGING TO GOOD

ETHAN

> Simple truth: "Hate what is evil; cling to what is good" (Romans 12:9). Today, I Am clinging to good. I'm His. All day.

HOW ABOUT YOU?

> Today, I Am...

DECEMBER 27

I AM PATIENCE, STRENGTH

TONY

Morning! A very happy, abundant day to you men. A familiar yet beautiful Scripture is found in Isaiah 40:31: "They who wait for the Lord shall renew their strength."

This is who I Am today: patience, strength.

Bless you both!

CURTIS

Tony, I see your patience and strength! God is using it through you all day long.

HOW ABOUT YOU?

Today, I Am...

DECEMBER 28

I AM CASTING ALL ANXIETY ON HIM

CURTIS

"Humble yourselves, therefore, under God's mighty hand, that He may lift you up in due time. Cast all your anxiety on him because He cares for you" (1 Peter 5:6-7).

Today I Am casting all anxiety on Him, who abundantly provides.

HOW ABOUT YOU?

Today, I Am...

DECEMBER 29

I AM AUTHENTIC

ETHAN

Good morning! Excited for today. This morning I read the verse about the speck in another's eye and the log in your own. The Message translation is awesome...

"It's this whole traveling road-show mentality all over again, playing a holier-than-thou part instead of just living your part" (Matthew 7:5).

Today, I Am authentic. My vision is on Him, and how I live my part for him. I see no specks but my own.

HOW ABOUT YOU?

Today, I Am...

DECEMBER 30

I AM FULLY EMBRACING GOD'S PURPOSE

CURTIS

"Many are the plans in a man's heart, but it is the Lord's purpose that prevails" (Proverbs 19:21).

Today I Am fully embracing God's purpose for my life.

HOW ABOUT YOU?

Today, I Am...

DECEMBER 31

I AM AUTHENTIC

TONY

Gents, reflecting on all our identity statements, I am struck in a new way by something I've always known, like seeing something new on a drive you do every day ...

All our identity statements reference back to God. Which is right. Our strength, our ability to overcome, our forgiveness, our love, our grace, our song, all of it is powerless without the Lord.

TONY

So today I state a single, all-encompassing identity statement: in Him I Am. Since God is God, His identity statement is "I AM who I AM" (Exodus 3:14).

For the believer, the closest and truest thing we can say is, "In Him I Am!" It embodies the oneness with God that we seek, which is how we were created to be: in His image.

HOW ABOUT YOU?

Today, I Am...

ACKNOWLEDGMENT:

We'd like to send a huge thank you for the inspiration of pastor Mark Batterson from the National Community Church in DC. It started when we all ready his fantastic *In a Pit with a Lion on a Snowy Day*. We've continued to enjoy all his books and be encouraged by all his sermons. When we read *The Circle Maker*, we agreed that we needed to draw "circles like Honi" around our biggest dreams and challenges.

Mark shares, "Drawing prayer circles around our dreams isn't just a mechanism whereby we accomplish great things for God. It's a mechanism whereby God accomplishes great things in us."

We sensed that there was far more to prayer, and to God's vision for our lives. We wanted to follow the example from the legend of Honi the Circle Maker—a man bold enough to draw a circle in the sand and not budge from inside it until God answered his prayers for his people. As part of our daily sharing we started "circling" each other, our families and our prayer requests. What we learned is that "circles" work.

Mark has challenged us to pray bigger prayers, and persist in them. And this book in your hands is an example of another circled prayer that has been answered!

ABOUT
CURTIS ESTES

Curtis Estes is Kristi's husband and Jordan, Vyvien, and Christian's dad. He is actively involved in the National Center for Fathering, a member of the Bel Air Presbyterian Church, and a supporter of the International Justice Mission. He has been a trustee for Spokane's Whitworth University for twelve years and is currently on the board at Pacifica Christian high school.

Curtis graduated from the University of Kansas with a degree in journalism in May 1991. Seven days later, he drove to Los Angeles, arriving on a Saturday. On Sunday, he attended Bel Air Presbyterian Church at the recommendation of a Jewish mentor of his. On Monday, he began his professional career with Northwestern Mutual.

He has been following the same routine every week for the past 30 years.

Curtis is a certified financial planner, CFP®, and the author of three prior books: *Your Life by Design: a Step-by-Step Guide to Creating a Bigger Future*, *Family First: How to Be a Hero at Home* and *Smart Money: Eight Strategies for Financial Security, Success, and Significance*.

ABOUT
ETHAN FREY

Ethan Frey is married to Jennifer, and they have three kids: Max, Macy and Mabel. Together, their lives are a beautiful, tender, daring, wonderful rolling ball of faith and fun.

Ethan graduated from Georgetown University in 1991. He loved his experience there, particularly competing in track and field. Ethan was blessed to be honored with the Robert A. Duffey Award, presented each year to the senior who best exhibits academic and athletic excellence. He went on to law school at Georgetown, graduating in 1995.

Shortly after graduating, at the age of 26, Ethan began a relationship with God. Ethan is now 52 years old, and he reflects often on how much better the second half of his life is—knowing God—than the first half (which was still pretty great!).

Today, Ethan is a private investor. He also is on the board of his local church and the Presidential Prayer Team, an organization committed to praying for the President of the United States and other government leaders, regardless of whether they are Republican or Democrat (both need prayer).

Ethan loves hiking, reading, finding good investment opportunities, traveling to new places, giving, serving, getting to know people, good wine, wasting time with friends, seeing movies in the theaters (with Milk Duds and popcorn...in the same bite!), golfing, and Christmas. Ethan especially loves his mornings with God, and every other time of day with family.

Finally, the dream in Ethan's heart is to launch a family camp where kids and adults can have outrageous fun and grow closer to God and each other through adventure.

ABOUT
TONY STACY

Tony is blessed to be the husband of his awesome wife, April, and father and stepfather to four wonderful young adults: Riley, Blake, Blair, and Brady.

He is actively involved in Highlands Church in Scottsdale, AZ, and currently serves as an ambassador of TGen, a non-profit organization based in Phoenix and an affiliate of City of Hope.

His business efforts are dedicated to 3rd Wave, a firm he founded in 2018 focused on the acquisition and development of four-star hotels in large metropolitan markets.

Made in the USA
Middletown, DE
27 November 2022